HOW TO BUILD, MAINTAIN, AND USE A COMPOST SYSTEM

Secrets and Techniques You Need to Know to Grow the Best Vegetables

REVISED 2ND EDITION

By Kelly Smith

HOW TO BUILD, MAINTAIN, AND USE A COMPOST SYSTEM:
Secrets and Techniques You Need to Know to Grow the Best Vegetables Revised 2nd Edition

Copyright © 2015 by Atlantic Publishing Group, Inc.
1405 SW 6th Ave. • Ocala, Florida 34471 • 800-814-1132 • 352-622-1875–Fax
Web site: www.atlantic-pub.com • E-mail: sales@atlantic-pub.com
SAN Number: 268-1250

Library of Congress Cataloging-in-Publication Data

Smith, Kelly M., 1969- author.
  How to build, maintain, and use a compost system : secrets and techniques you need to know to grow the best vegetables / by: Kelly Smith. -- Revised 2nd edition.
    pages cm
  ISBN 978-1-62023-013-8 (alk. paper) -- ISBN 1-62023-013-5 (alk. paper) 1. Compost. 2. Vegetable gardening. I. Title.
S661.S646 2015
631.8'75--dc23
                        2015023954

2ND EDITION EDITOR: Melissa Shortman • mfigueroa@atlantic-pub.com
COVER DESIGN: Meg Buchner • megadesn@mchsi.com

Printed in the United States

Printed on Recycled Paper

Reduce. Reuse.
RECYCLE.

A decade ago, Atlantic Publishing signed the Green Press Initiative. These guidelines promote environmentally friendly practices, such as using recycled stock and vegetable-based inks, avoiding waste, choosing energy-efficient resources, and promoting a no-pulping policy. We now use 100-percent recycled stock on all our books. The results: in one year, switching to post-consumer recycled stock saved 24 mature trees, 5,000 gallons of water, the equivalent of the total energy used for one home in a year, and the equivalent of the greenhouse gases from one car driven for a year.

Over the years, we have adopted a number of dogs from rescues and shelters. First there was Bear and after he passed, Ginger and Scout. Now, we have Kira, another rescue. They have brought immense joy and love not just into our lives, but into the lives of all who met them.

We want you to know a portion of the profits of this book will be donated in Bear, Ginger and Scout's memory to local animal shelters, parks, conservation organizations, and other individuals and nonprofit organizations in need of assistance.

— Douglas & Sherri Brown,
President & Vice-President of Atlantic Publishing

ACKNOWLEDGEMENTS

I'd like to thank the following people for their willingness to provide case study information: Andrea Zuercher, Carrie Bennett, John Cossham, Kimberly Roy, Kimberly Wolterman, Linda Stephenson, Marianne Carlson, Robert and Debra Post, and Sara Estep. It was a pleasure to work with you all. I'd like to add extra thanks to Robert Post for going out of his way to provide instructions and accompanying photographs for the barrel composter section.

I would also like to thank all the amateur composting enthusiasts who spend a lot of time and effort to share their knowledge online through blogs, videos, and tutorials. Your work is appreciated and admired.

TABLE OF CONTENTS

INTRODUCTION

WHY COMPOST?

> "Garbage becomes rose. Rose becomes compost. Everything is in transformation. Even permanence is impermanent."
>
> — Buddhist monk, Thich Nhat Hanh

The quote above is from Thich Nhat Hanh, founder of the Unified Buddhist Church in France. His teachings focus on the interconnectedness of all things and often reflect the environmentally minded, earth-caring aspect of composting. The interrelationship of "garbage" and "roses," or more likely manure and vegetables, has been apparent to farmers for centuries. Composting is probably as old as human agriculture. There are references to composting recorded on clay tablets in Mesopotamia going back to at least 500 B.C. The Bible, the Talmud, and other early written sources mention the agricultural use of manure and other compost-like substances, so composting was well known even from early times.

The use of compost as a soil enricher continued until the 19th century when commercially produced chemical fertilizers were developed. These fertilizers were an important part of the formation of modern agribusiness because they were not as labor-intensive as making compost and could support enormous commercial crops. The downside of commercial fertilizers was not apparent for some time, but eventually it was discovered that the runoff of nitrogen and phosphorous from fertilized fields caused algae blooms and subsequent fish kills and dead zones in ponds, lakes, and rivers. Dead zones develop when algae overgrows and uses up all the oxygen in a body of water, killing the fish and other aquatic creatures. Nitrates in the groundwater supply can lead to the potentially fatal blue baby syndrome, which is an illness in newborns that decreases the capacity of their hemoglobin to carry oxygen. As more and more problems associated with overuse of commercial fertilizers have been discovered, more and more people are turning to natural alternatives and are using compost. Even commercial organic farms use compost. The U.S. Department of Agriculture administers the rules and guidelines for the use of compost in organic farms. These guidelines are very specific about what can and cannot be used in compost for organic farming and closely mirror what a home gardener would use.

Many people compost at home for purely pragmatic reasons; they want organic nutrients for their gardens, and composting is the most inexpensive way to obtain them. Making compost can be free if you use an open compost pile or an existing container and tools. This can save money spent on fertilizers, potting soil, and commercially available soil amendments because compost can significantly reduce the need for all three items. This book discusses the benefits of using compost as a soil amendment and tells you how to build and care for your own compost system to yield rich compost that can feed your plants and nourish seedlings. Compost can also save you money on your waste disposal bill. Food waste makes up about 7 percent of the garbage sent to landfills every year. By composting all your plant-based garbage, you could make a dent in the amount of trash you throw out and might be able to get a smaller bin and a reduced rate from your trash collection company.

Other people compost for the good of the planet. Taking the waste from our meals and the trimmings from our gardens and turning them into rich soil amendments that will help grow the next crop of food is an excellent way to remove products from the waste stream and put them to good use. Most people are already well-versed in recycling bottles, cans, paper, and other items that we used to think of as garbage. Composting is a way to do the same with our organic "garbage," thus easing the strain on, and saving us the cost of transporting our waste to, already overburdened landfills. Unlike commercial fertilizers, composting also puts organic additives into the soil that help plants grow bigger and stronger and stay healthier. Compost can not only feed plants, but it can also prevent many common plant diseases. At the same time, compost does no harm to the environment the way commercially produced chemical fertilizers and pesticides can. Overusing chemical fertilizers can strip soil of fertility and poison worms and other valuable creatures. Overusing pesticides can lead to resistance in pests, making those that are left heartier and defeating the whole purpose of pesticides in the first place.

Whether you are reading this book to find a cheaper way to feed your garden, or a way to help the environment by cutting back on the waste coming out of your kitchen, you will find something helpful here. Think of compost not as an end product, but as part of a never-ending cycle as Thich Nhat Hanh points out. The compost becomes food, and the food becomes compost.

Making compost is fun and easy.

CHAPTER I

LET US BEGIN
WITH THE BASICS

What is Composting?

To protect the environment this man puts kitchen scraps into the bin to reuse the compost on his garden.

At its most basic level, **composting** is the rotting of organic (plant-based) matter. More formally, composting is the process of breaking organic matter down into its primary components so the resulting **humus**, which is the rich, dark organic soil made of decomposed plant and animal matter, can be used to fertilize plants and amend the soil. Composting happens in nature when the rain wets fallen leaves, animal droppings, and other materials on the ground. Fungi and microorganisms grow in this mixture and consume the material, breaking it down into component parts, which results in compost. Gardeners can mimic and accelerate natural composting through the judicious application of some simple concepts. Proper balance between wet and dry materials; moisture and oxygen; and nitrogen and carbon will turn yard and kitchen waste into a moist, fertile soil amendment in a matter of months. Composting is quite simple and, after a system is established, takes minimal time and effort to maintain.

How Composting Benefits your Garden

Moist garden humus compost with small wood chips, bark and sticks.

Compost is beneficial to all gardens, large or small, whether you are growing vegetables, herbs, fruit, flowers, or just grass and trees. It is also useful in potted houseplants and container gardens. Because you choose what materials to put into your compost system, you can control exactly what is put on your garden and, if you grow your own fruits, herbs, and vegetables, into your meals. Compost uses gardening waste that would otherwise be disposed of or burned. You can use almost every healthy plant and plant part in a compost system. Instead of raking up leaves and

Many state and local governments are developing programs for composting as well as mulching.

grass clippings to be hauled away, put them in your compost. When a plant dies or vegetables spoil, put them in the compost instead of in the trash that has to be trucked away to landfills.

Using compost will reduce the amount of watering you have to do and will keep your garden soil evenly moist, protecting delicate plants in very hot or dry weather. It will also help amend heavy clay soils so water will not pool and flood your plants. Compost contains bacteria and microbes that create natural antibiotics. These substances can help prevent many common plant diseases and help you grow healthier flowers and vegetables.

Composting is good for your garden, for the environment, and for your pocket book. Here are some reasons you should begin to compost:

- Compost contains beneficial bacteria and microorganisms that contribute to soil health, and it contains the basic building blocks of plants — nitrogen and carbon. It also contains a variety of micronutrients that are vital to the health of your plants. These micronutrients include boron, copper, iodine, manganese, molybdenum, and zinc, and all are important to the health of your plants.

- Compost provides a home for insects and worms, and these creatures play an important role in producing compost.

- Compost helps keep soil at a neutral pH, which is healthier for most plants. PH is a measure of acidity and alkalinity. On the pH scale, 7 represents neutrality and the lower a number, the higher the acidity. The higher the number on the scale, the higher the alkalinity. For example, soil with a pH of 2.4 is more acidic than soil with a pH of 5.3. If soil has a reading of 9.3, it is more alkaline than soil with a pH of 7.5. A pH reading between 6 and 7 is advantageous for your garden because soil at this pH level makes beneficial nutrients such as nitrogen, phosphorus, and potassium available to plants.

> Soil pH is a measurement of the acidity or alkalinity of a soil. Soil pH is critical because it affects the health of plants. Before plants can use a nutrient, it must be dissolved in soil water (most nutrients dissolve best when the soil is slightly acidic to neutral). The good news is ... Soil pH is easy to check and can be altered / corrected.

Sample pH scale   Neutral

← Strongly Acid	Medium Acid	Slightly Acid	Very Slightly Acid	Very Slightly Alkaline	Slightly Alkaline	Medium Alkaline	Strongly Alkaline →

1.0   5.5   6.0   6.5   7.0   7.5   8.0   8.5   14.0

- Unlike commercially produced fertilizers that provide a big hit of a limited number of nutrients all at once, compost provides steady, ongoing fertilization by releasing a much wider variety of nutrients slowly into the soil, feeding the plants for a longer time at a much lower cost. While compost cannot completely replace commercial fertilizers (because it is hard to control exactly what nutrients are in a given batch of compost or in what concentrations), it can help lower the amount of fertilizer you have to use to achieve the same result.

- Compost improves the consistency of soil because it creates small clumps of materials known as **aggregates**. These aggregates create small gaps in thick clay soil, allowing water and oxygen to seep down to plant roots. In dry, sandy soil, these aggregates help hold water, making the soil more nutritious for plants and decreasing the amount of watering needed for gardens, flower beds, and lawns.

- Compost binds with toxins like lead and cadmium so that plants cannot consume them, keeping these poisons out of the food chain. Tests conducted on soil contaminated with oily waste found that applying compost to the contaminated soil led to a significant reduction in toxic chemicals. Compost cleans up toxins because it binds with them on a molecular level. According to the website Composter Connection (**www.composterconnection. com/site/introduction.html**), compost can remediate (or decontaminate) polluted soil. It traps some toxins in the soil and helps plants consume others. By harvesting these contaminated plants and their roots you can literally pull the contaminants out of the ground.

- Regular use of compost can suppress some plant diseases such as club root in cabbages, white rot in onions, brown rot in potatoes, mildew, and potato blight. Some diseases, such as potato blight, can wipe out entire crops. This happened in the 1840s in Ireland, Scotland, and parts of Europe, but if you catch most diseases early, you can eradicate most of them by removing and destroying the diseased plants. It is easy to tell which plants are infected; they are the ones that are droopy, do not produce blossoms or fruit, or are visibly discolored, moldy, or dying.

- Recycling waste material from your kitchen and garden means you do not have to spend as much money on trash removal or recycling services. The nutrients you create with compost provide free, natural fertilizer for your plants and vegetables.

• Fruits and vegetables that are grown in nutrient-depleted soils contain fewer vitamins, minerals, and micronutrients that humans need for good health. Growing your own produce in soil amended with rich compost can improve the health of you and your family.

How Composting Benefits the Environment

A municipal composting project.

The U.S. Environmental Protection Agency (EPA) estimates that about 13 percent of municipal solid waste is made up of yard waste and trimmings. (Municipal solid waste is trash thrown away by households and does not normally include commercial or hazardous waste.) This 13 percent accounts for about 33 million tons of yard waste being trucked to landfills in the United States. Not only is this an unnecessary expense for cities and towns, but the fossil fuels burned to transport this waste to the landfill also contribute to global climate change. Food scraps and kitchen waste make up almost 12 percent of municipal solid waste, accounting for 32 million tons of trash per year. Throwing away these clean, biodegradable materials instead of including them in your compost pile wastes space in landfills. More than eight percent of the waste that each person generates each day, which amounts to more than 140 pounds per person annually, can be recovered for composting. Composting is a simple, enjoyable way to use yard and kitchen waste. It saves money for the homeowner and the municipality, and it relieves congestion on the roads and the use of fossil fuels that contaminate our air.

Composting has many benefits to the environment.

- Composting plant-based materials, rather than letting them rot in a landfill, helps keep gases like methane out of the atmosphere. **Methane** is a by-product of anaerobic decomposition, which is what occurs in a landfill. In an active aerobic compost pile, almost no methane should be released.

- Composting also results in less carbon dioxide gas added to the atmosphere because the microbes in the compost consume most of the carbon and release only a small amount of it into the air as CO_2.

- Compost provides a simple and green alternative to using **peat moss**. Peat is a non-renewable resource that is dug up and sold to gardeners to enrich garden soil. Peat helps soil retain water and allows water to drain so that garden soil is neither too wet nor too dry. Removing peat from its natural habitat can prevent the wetlands from performing their natural function, which is to filter toxins from watersheds. Compost, which is also porous, decayed organic matter, provides all the benefits of peat with none of the drawbacks or cost to you or the environment.

- Compost provides essential nutrients, allowing the gardener to grow healthy plants without using commercial fertilizers. This allows the gardener to grow fruits and vegetables free of potentially harmful chemicals and saves the energy and money that would otherwise be spent making, buying, and transporting fertilizer.

- There is much less runoff of potentially harmful chemicals from fertilizers into streams and rivers. This runoff can result in the overgrowth of algae in pond, lakes, and rivers and can lead to the death of fish and other aquatic creatures. The runoff can also introduce harmful nitrates into the groundwater supply, which affects human health.

- Compost does not have to be manufactured and transported hundreds or thousands of miles to the point of use, the way commercial fertilizers are. Normally compost is produced near to where it is used (either in the garden or at least in the same community), saving energy and fossil fuels.

Common Myths About Composting

- Composting is difficult.

False. Composting is merely the act of assembling organic materials into a pile and letting them decompose. You can get very fancy with gadgets, measurements and scientific data, but at its base, composting is just human-assisted decomposition of plant materials, and it can be as simple as piling things up and leaving them alone.

- Compost piles always smell bad.

False. Compost piles that contain the right balance of wet and dry ingredients and that are turned or mixed regularly will not smell. In fact, fresh, completed compost smells identical to fresh, fertile soil.

- Composting is just for people who live in the country.

False. Anyone who can assemble the materials and put them into a container can compost. There are composting systems that take up as little as 2 square feet of floor or cabinet space.

- All compost bins are the same.

False. Different styles of compost bins are made because composters' circumstances differ. Some styles can handle meat and fat scraps; some handle only plant material. Some keep out vermin; others work best indoors. There is a style of bin for every need.

- Any kind of worm will work for vermicomposting (creating compost using worms).

False. High temperatures in a compost bin can kill Common earthworms (and so they usually flee the bin when it gets too hot). They also do not do well in the rich environment of a vermicomposting bin. Only a few species of worms are typically used in composting, and these should be purchased from a reputable dealer.

• You cannot put color paper or inks in compost.

False. Contemporary inks and paper products contain levels of heavy metals and hydrocarbons that are well below the limits set by the EPA, and these substances break down quickly in the compost pile.

As you can see, many myths you may have heard about composting are not true. Composting is a relatively simple, fun way to make something valuable out of your trash. It is good for your wallet, your plants, and the planet as a whole.

About This Book

This book will give you simple instructions for composting no matter where you live or what type of garden you have. Whether you have a large vegetable garden or a small collection of houseplants, using compost will improve the health and beauty of your plants. You will also learn how to make your own compost containers, how to compost with worms, how to make compost tea, how and where to use compost in your garden, and how composting can help the environment on a large scale and make your own little corner of the world healthier. You will find case studies from people all over the United States and one from the United Kingdom. These people all compost at home and were happy to describe how and why they compost, what they enjoy about it, what difficulties they encountered, and how they overcame them.

Composting is a good idea not only financially, but also for your soil, your family, your community, and the world as a whole. In this book you will learn:

- The benefits of composting

- How composting can lead to healthier vegetables

- How composting can improve the health of your plants

- The science behind composting

- What items can and cannot safely be composted

- How to build your own outdoor compost bin

- How to compost indoors or outdoors with various kinds of commercial bins

- How to compost with worms (vermicomposting)

- How to tell when your compost is ready to use

- How and where to use compost and compost tea

- Ways to manage some of the problems that can arise with composting

f you are new to composting, consider reading at least those two chapters before skipping ahead. If you are a somewhat experienced composter, feel free to jump the sections that interest you.

Note on terminology: Throughout most of this book, the term "organic" is used to describe items that are derived from living organisms, not necessarily items that are free of chemicals, pesticides, and fertilizers. This is because the produce that most people purchase at the grocery store has been grown with the use of some chemicals, and not all of those chemicals will be removed through the process of composting.

CHAPTER 2

GETTING STARTED

"My whole life has been spent waiting for an epiphany, a manifestation of God's presence, the kind of transcendent, magical experience that lets you see your place in the big picture. And that is what I had with my first compost heap. I love compost, and I believe that composting can save not the entire world, but a good portion of it."

— Bette Midler in an interview with the *LA Times*

Composting is simple, but there are a few questions to ask yourself before you start.

- What kind of system is right for me?

- Where will I put it?

- What items can I compost?

- What items should I avoid?

•   Where can I get compost ingredients?

This chapter will answer all these questions and more. The first thing you will need to explore are the different kinds of composting systems available so you can decide which type is best for your situation. Below is an overview of the types of compost systems available. Each type of system will be described in detail in later chapters, but this overview will give you the information you need to figure out what will work for you.

Types of Compost Systems

Compost heaps or piles

One type of system you can use is a simple compost pile or heap. This is probably most commonly known kind of compost system, and it is the easiest composting method if you have the space for it. A compost heap is a pile of compost material exposed to the elements, not contained in a bin. It is easy to add to it as you accumulate ingredients, so you do not have to collect a large amount of material before starting to build your pile. You can easily mix the ingredients because the pile is not contained. Use a pitchfork to toss items and combine them. This type of compost system can also take the form of a **windrow**, a long pile of material that is turned by hand (for small windrows) or by machine (for large farm-scale windrows).

Any open bin or pile may get some weed seeds blown into it and will also be more susceptible to rain, which will leach nutrients out of it. This leaching of nutrients is one main drawback of an open-heap system. Ideally, you want the heap to retain as many nutrients as possible until you are ready to use the compost in your garden. The contents may also blow and scatter around the yard if the pile is not covered. Covering an uncontained heap with a blanket or piece of carpeting is a good way to prevent the compost materials from blowing away and to keep the pile warm, aiding decomposition. If you cover the heap, make sure to use a breathable cover, not something like a plastic tarp that will trap moisture and cause mildew.

This method is best suited to rural areas because it does not have the neat and orderly look sometimes required in urban settings,

and it can take up quite a bit of space. It may also be considered "unsightly" by neighbors, so you may have to situate it in an out-of-the-way spot or behind a fence.

Compost heap made of unused vegetables to recycle.

Compost bins

You can use a single bin or a series of three bins made of wood, concrete blocks, or hay or straw bales. These bins contain the compost ingredients, making for a tidier appearance more

Example of a simple rustic compost bin.

suitable in semi-rural or suburban neighborhoods. The materials used to build the bins can help keep the compost warm and can sometimes provide additional nutrients, as in the case of hay or straw bales, or wooden bins lined with cardboard. Bins must be stirred or turned with a pitchfork or shovel. Normally this type of system is large enough even for a very active gardener, but the bins can fill up, and you may have to store ingredients separately until the time is right to add them. Typically, the first bin in the common three-bin system is used to store materials as they are acquired. The second bin is used to combine the materials and begin the composting process and the third bin is used to finish off the composting process. Materials are forked from one bin to the next as time goes on, so you get a continuous supply of compost.

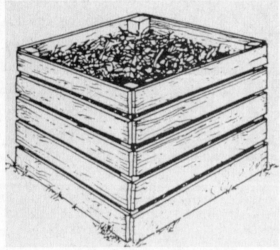

Example of a simple compost bin.
Courtesy of USDA.

Holes or trenches

You can use a hole or trench in the ground for composting. This method can work anywhere as long as you have dirt to dig in. The compost ingredients can be buried if you do not need the finished compost, or left in an open trench if you want to create compost to spread on a garden. Some forms of trench composting use plywood sides to contain the pile of compost above ground level, where it is then chopped and mixed using a **rototiller**. (A rototiller is a landscaping implement with engine-powered rotating blades used to lift and turn over soil.) *This method is described in Chapter 3 under Wood Trench Composting.* Composting in a hole can attract animals, so you will have to take some precautions to discourage them, such as covering the compost with dirt or covering the hole with a heavy lid. This composting method may be unsightly to neighbors and is not for everyone.

Cone digester systems

You can use a digester system where the compost itself ends up underground in a perforated bin while a plastic cone extends above ground level, allowing you to easily add material until it is full. You must move this kind of system periodically as the underground bin fills with solid waste. Liquid waste will soak into the surrounding soil and insects and small burrowing animals may make off with some, but probably not all, of the solid waste. This kind of system will only enrich the small area where the compost is buried. If the underground container is not rat-proof, you may end up with a rat problem because they can chew into the container to eat the scraps. This kind of system is not designed to make compost to spread on a garden. Like the hole system, the compost is left underground.

Rotating or tumbling barrels

You can either purchase or make a rotating or tumbling barrel to make compost. *(Instructions for making a barrel composter are included in Chapter 3.)* These systems are fully enclosed, so you do not need to worry about attracting animals. They also provide some protection from the elements and are easy to fill. Barrels are designed to allow air into the compost, and the tumbling action helps mix the ingredients. These systems come with a variety of different mechanisms for turning them. Some use a rotating handle with gears to assist in turning, and some are turned by pushing on them with your foot or by pushing and pulling them end-over-end by hand. Some models (especially the upright tumbling barrels that must be turned end-over-end) can be difficult to turn, and even more difficult to empty on your own, so you should take that into consideration if you will be the only one doing the work.

Stationary bins

Example of a stationary bin.

You can use a stationary compost container. These are plastic bins, often provided by cities or towns, and come in a wide variety of shapes, colors, and designs. You must stir the ingredients manually to introduce air into the compost. These systems are very neat and are acceptable in most settings where you have some amount of yard space. Some types of stationary bins have no bottoms, which prevent liquids from building up and drowning the bacteria, but this also means that the ground around the bin may become saturated. Consider this when placing your bin. Outdoor **vermicomposting** bins, which use worms to digest the compost ingredients, are also of this type and can be used in some climates where the weather is temperate and not prone to extreme cold or heat because these conditions will kill the worms. *(Vermicomposting is discussed in detail in Chapter 7.)*

Indoor systems

There are many types of systems meant for indoor use, including vermicomposting systems that use microbe-infused additives and systems that electrically heat and automatically tumble the compost ingredients. These can be used in homes, condominiums, and apartments and generally take up little space. The downside is that they may lead to odors or fly infestations if not properly maintained. They are very handy for people who have physical difficulties and cannot work with an outdoor compost system, and they drastically reduce the volume of kitchen waste sent to landfills.

How Big is a Compost Pile?

When most people think of an outdoor compost bin, they may envision anything from a giant pile of leaves, scraps, and random garden clippings to a small, tidy container with kitchen scraps and shredded paper. Compost that is contained in a bin or tumbler is only as large as the container the compost is housed in.

The size of a compost heap varies depending on the amount of space you have, the amount of ingredients you can assemble, and the amount of time and effort you want to invest in maintaining it. The typical size of an outdoor compost heap is approximately 4 feet by 4 feet and 5 to 6 feet high. This is large enough to get very warm, consume a large quantity of waste, and is manageable for most people to turn. When this book mentions "large compost piles," you should envision this the size compost system. Smaller piles will also work, but they will not get as hot and cannot consume as much waste. Smaller piles are much easier to turn and may be preferred by some gardeners. Again, it is up to you to determine how much you can handle and how much compost you reasonably need to produce for your purposes.

Choosing a System

Now that you know the general kinds of compost systems available, you will have to make some decisions before you get started with composting. You can compost no matter where you live, but the kind of system you use and where you put it will depend on the kind of home and neighborhood you live in, available space, and how much you are willing to work or spend on your compost system.

The type of system you choose should fit your lifestyle and not be a burden. Composting is fun, and when you see garbage almost magically transformed into soil, you will wonder why you did not start sooner.

The following are some questions you should ask yourself to discover what kind of composting system will work for you:

- How much space do you have available?

- How much time do you have to tend to your compost?

- How much money do you want to spend to get started?

- Do you want to make a large amount of compost (enough for a garden), or only a little (enough for container plants)?

- How much yard and kitchen waste do you normally produce that can be used for compost?

- Do you want to do standard composting or vermicomposting?

- Do you want to do more than one kind of composting, for example, outdoor composting in the summer and indoor composting in the winter months?

Answering these questions will tell you what sort of system might be best for you. *Chapters 3, 4, and 8 contain detailed information on creating and using various compost systems*, and the table below may help you choose the kind of system that is right for you.

	Compost bin (indoor)	Vermicompost (indoor)	Compost bin (outdoor)	Compost heap or pile (outdoor)
Rural	✓	✓	✓	✓
Suburban	✓	✓	✓	✓
City	✓	✓	✓	
Condo	✓	✓		
Apartment	✓	✓		

If you are in doubt about which kind of system you prefer, you may want to start with a smaller or easier system. While large three-bin outdoor systems are commonly seen in composting books and websites, they do take a lot of space and energy to maintain. A small in-kitchen composter or a stationary outdoor bin may be the best way for you to get started. Only you know your limitations and how much effort you will put into composting, so do not let yourself be overwhelmed by all the different choices.

Can I compost?

Almost anyone can compost. In addition to the kind of area you live in, the second biggest determining factor in what kind of system to choose is the amount of effort you are able to invest. Composting will occur even if you invest very little effort. You can pile up the compost materials, do nothing, and in a year or two, you will have compost. But if you want to make an effort and create compost in a few months, decide how much time you have for composting, how often you can tend to it, and how physically fit you are. If you spend time in your garden every day, you will have more than enough time for composting. If you work all day and only get into the garden on weekends, you can still compost using any method you like, provided you have the space. If you are physically disabled or live in a small apartment or condominium, your options are more limited, but you can compost using an indoor system.

The kind of system you use will depend mainly on cost, location, and effort, so take all those things into consideration when deciding which one is right for you.

What kind of system can I afford?

Compost systems come in a wide variety of types and price ranges from free ones your city or town may provide, to extensive homemade compost bins that can take up a lot of space and require a small initial monetary investment, to large commercially available systems with all the bells and whistles that cost several hundred dollars. You can compost with nothing more than a trash bag, or you can build several types of compost heaps, bins, trenches, and piles to compost different materials for different uses. Any method that keeps waste out of the landfill and provides you with quality compost is beneficial.

Where will the compost system go?

If you have a large rural property, options for where to locate the compost system are limited only by how far you want to walk to fill it, tend it, and empty it. You can locate your compost bin or pile anywhere on your property. For outdoor systems, you may want your compost either near your kitchen so you can easily fill the compost bin or container with kitchen scraps, or near your garden so you will not have to carry the finished compost too far. The ideal location is a level, dry, shaded area that is easy to water (within reach of a garden hose is good) and easy to transport compost to your garden. Place your compost pile on well-drained soil so it does not flood, which will stop the composting process. Never place a compost pile on a solid surface like concrete, pavement, or plastic; that will inhibit contact with natural microbes in the soil and may prevent proper drainage.

If you live in a city or urban area, you may have to balance your need for easy access with your neighbor's desire not to look at a compost pile. You may be able to erect a fence around your pile to screen it from the neighbor's view if necessary. You will also have to beware of runoff if you use an outdoor system. The liquid that drains from an active compost pile may contain ammonia or a surplus of nitrogen, depending on what is in your compost and how healthy the pile is. If this liquid runs into your neighbor's yard, it may kill the grass or other plants. Your neighbors also may not want a mucky spot on their property courtesy of your compost's runoff. To avoid this, you can grade the ground so that any runoff that occurs flows into your own yard. **Grading** is the process of leveling the ground so that it slopes smoothly in one direction or the other. You can do this with a shovel and rake or with a tractor with a blade, depending on how much soil you need to move.

You can also start the compost pile in a hole or depression in the soil, but then you also run the risk of the pile flooding. Flooding will not only wash away valuable nutrients, but also can drown the aerobic bacteria and cause the pile to become anaerobic, leaving you with a puddle of smelly muck. If you do decide to compost in a hole, realize that the compost will best be buried there, and you will not be able to dig it up easily to use in other areas. The best location for an outdoor compost pile is on well-drained, level ground, far enough from property lines that your neighbors will not have a problem with it.

Aerobic means air breathing. You want to encourage these bacteria and microorganisms to live in your compost because when they breathe, they release nothing more than carbon dioxide. **Anaerobic** means non-air breathing. These microorganisms release nasty-smelling gases, including ammonia and hydrogen sulfide, which makes anaerobic compost stink. Aerobic composting is generally preferred, although there are some situations where you might want to let things decompose in an air-tight environment, such as when killing weeds or making trash-bag compost, as described in Chapter 3.

If you live in a condominium with a tiny yard or in an apartment with no yard, balcony, or deck, you can still compost. There are small, enclosed systems available that take up little space. There are even indoor systems designed for use year-round that do not require any outdoor space. You can use the resulting compost in container gardens, donate it to community gardens, or sell it to other gardeners.

Are there local ordinances to account for?

There may be local restrictions on the presence and placement of compost bins or piles. These rules generally are put in place as the result of composting gone bad, such as when an inexperienced composter lets his or her pile go anaerobic, causing an awful smell. Well-meaning but misinformed people who assume that all compost stinks or is attractive to pests may also encourage anti-composting rules in their towns. While it is true that compost may attract vermin if it is in an open bin or not kept in proper balance, a properly maintained compost system, especially one that is enclosed in some kind of bin or container, will be no more attractive to pests than the average neighborhood garbage can, and probably less so, since it will not contain meat, fat, bones, or other items that scavengers will go after. While small creatures such as mice may still make their way into some types of bins, they will not stay if you keep it hot and turn it regularly.

Some neighbors may complain because they do not want to look at your compost heap, and there may be local ordinances against having one in certain areas of your property, so it is a good idea to check with local authorities to see if there are any rules or guidelines about composting in your area. If you have municipal trash services, that will be the best place to inquire. If not, a call to your town or city hall should point you in the right direction.

Some cities pick up compost material from residents' homes in much the same way that they pick up trash and recyclable materials. Some provide a central drop-off point where residents can bring their compost. Most cities that encourage recycling and composting will provide supplies, or at least information, to help you get started. They also generally make the community-created compost available for purchase to residents. This does several things. First, it keeps organic material out of the landfill. Second, it encourages people to think about what they are throwing away. Third, it provides inexpensive organic compost for the city and its residents, beautifying gardens and parks, and leading to a healthier environment overall. Depending on where you live, you may contact your local trash collection company, county extension agency, or town or city hall for information.

Some municipalities offer composting programs to residents, and in some cities composting is strongly encouraged. Cities such as San Francisco have started to collect compostable materials from residents and businesses to compost on a large scale. The city is able to compost items that a home composter cannot, such as greasy cardboard, meat, and bones. The finished compost is then sold to businesses, such as farms and vineyards. These programs vary across the country and around the world, so you will want to check the rules in your area. Some may charge a fee for the service while others, like San Francisco, levy fines if waste is not properly sorted.

If your city or town does not already collect kitchen and yard

scraps for composting, you may think about championing the effort or starting your own composting group. Even if you just start small with friends and neighbors, you can help the environment and end up with nearly free compost.

Once you have chosen a compost system, the next question to consider is what items you can include in your compost system.

Small kitchen recycling container.

What Can I Compost?

You can turn almost everything that grows in your garden and many of the food scraps from your kitchen into compost. There are two major classes of composting materials: **Green waste** — items such as kitchen scraps, fresh grass clippings, cuttings from plants, green manure (plants like clover that are rich in nitrogen fixers), new-fallen leaves, and animal manure; and **brown waste**, which includes paper and cardboard, branches, twigs, tree bark, wood chips or sawdust, and dried grass or leaves. Later in this chapter, you will find an extensive list of ingredients that can be used in composting.

As with your own diet, the greater the variety of materials you put into your pile or bin, the greater the variety of nutrients you will have in the finished compost and the healthier it will be. Like any healthy diet, it is all about balance and variety. For example, a compost pile that has nothing but wood chips, which are very high in carbon, will take many years to break down. There has to be enough nitrogen-rich green waste to provide food for the micro-organisms that eat the compost. **Microorganisms** are microscopic creatures, such as bacteria and fungi that break the scraps down into their component parts. The balance between the amount of green materials and the amount of brown materials is important.

Know that you need to include both green and brown waste to make your compost work at peak efficiency.

Kitchen scraps ready for the composting bin.

Yard and garden waste

If you have any kind of yard or garden, you have waste materials you can use in compost. You can compost leaves, spent plants or blossoms, and clippings from trees, shrubs, and hedges. You can also compost spoiled fruit and vegetables, along with the vines and plants they grow on. If you keep farm animals, their manure

will make a great addition to your compost, as will old hay or straw, especially any that has been used for bedding. You can even compost the debris from your gutters during spring and fall yard clean up.

Ready for the compost pile.

Green materials

You can collect green materials, also called wet materials, from your garden throughout the spring, summer, and fall. These items are high in nitrogen and decompose very quickly. When you mow the lawn, you can rake the clippings into your compost pile. Be cautious about adding too many fresh clippings to a small compost bin because they will quickly burn off available brown materials and turn the contents of the bin to muck. If you have only a small compost bin, it will be best to leave the clippings on the lawn to act as natural mulch. When you deadhead your flowers, toss the spent blossoms in the compost. **Deadheading** is the process of plucking dead blossoms from flowering plants to prolong the flowering period in perennials by preventing them from going to seed.

If worms, bugs, or other pests spoil the fruits and vegetables in your garden, toss the ruined items into the compost. If you are lucky enough to live on or near a horse, chicken, or cattle farm, you can ask the farmers for the animals' manure. Many individuals are very happy to let you have all the manure you can shovel, but some larger farms charge for the privilege. They know the value of manure to a gardener. Other green materials you might use include wool, feathers from poultry, and hair from pets. These items are all high in nitrogen and will compost well.

Some weeds contain valuable minerals because their taproots can pull nutrients from deep under the soil where garden plants cannot reach. A **taproot** is a large root that grows straight down with smaller roots branching off it. Think of a carrot and you have the general idea of what a taproot is. These weeds are called **dynamic accumulators** because they gather up helpful nutrients from several inches under the soil. These nutrients are valuable in compost, and it is possible to safely compost non-pernicious weeds, as discussed later in this chapter. **Pernicious** weeds are fast growing

 and destructive to other plants. Weeds like thistle, bindweed, morning glory, and Bermuda grass are common examples of weeds that are generally considered pernicious.

Fresh green grass ready to use for composting.

Brown materials

You can collect brown materials, also called dry materials, throughout the growing season and even during winter. These items are high in carbon and decompose much more slowly than green materials. Every time you prune a bush or shrub, collect fallen branches or bark after a windstorm, or rake up dried leaves, you can contribute to the compost. A large concentration of brown or carbon-rich materials will take a very long time to break down, so these materials must be cut or chopped into small pieces. Dry hay or other dried grasses, as long as they are finely chopped, can also be put into the compost. Many people use a machete to chop

long grasses and other fibrous plant material. A large kitchen knife or a small hatchet will also work. Chopping these elements will allow them to mix more thoroughly with the other ingredients and break down faster.

Brown leaves ready for the compost pile.

Non-living items such as wood ash, sand, lime, stone dust, finished compost, or garden soil may also be added to the compost although only very small amounts are needed.

- Wood ash (such as ashes left over from a campfire or fireplace) provides potash (also called potassium carbonate) and can be layered into compost every 18 inches or so. Use only a small sprinkling and mix it in well. Do not mix it directly with manure because the potash will leach nitrogen from the manure. Plants use potash to make chlorophyll, which allows them to transform sunlight into energy.

- Worms use grit in their gullet to grind up the plant material they eat, so a small amount of sand in compost will not hurt and might be beneficial. **Grit** is small, sharp granules of rock, and a **gullet** is part of the worm's digestive system where food is pre-processed before continuing down into their intestines. Coarse or "sharp" sand

helps increase aeration in compost by providing larger pores in the finished compost for air and water to flow through. This can be useful when adding compost to clay soils. Sand does not provide any nutrients.

Worms use grit in their gullet to grind up the plant material they eat.

- Some people add lime to their compost to counteract acidity if they have a lot of acidic materials such as pine needles and coffee grounds in their compost. It can also be added to worm bins or compost heaps if they get wet and smelly or too acidic. If using limestone in a worm bin, make sure to add only a very small amount and to stir it in well over several days, because it can react with the compost and release carbon dioxide, which will suffocate the

worms. Lime will also leach nitrogen from a compost pile and can cause the release of ammonia and nitrogen gas if it is sprinkled directly onto fresh manure, so it should be used sparingly, if at all. See the following for more in-

Coffee grounds and eggshells ready for composting.

formation before deciding whether or not to add limestone to your compost.

SHOULD YOU ADD LIME TO YOUR COMPOST?

Lime used in agriculture is a fine, white powder made from ground up limestone. It is made up mostly of calcium carbonate and is used to decrease acidity in soil. There are other kinds of lime, such as pickling lime and slaked lime, but these have a different chemical makeup and should not be used in composting.

Because lime can cause problems in a compost heap (it can leach nitrogen and release carbon dioxide), it is best to wait until a few weeks after you have enriched your soil with finished compost and then test the soil's pH level. If the soil is still too acidic, add lime directly to the soil to bring it closer to neutral. Lime can be purchased at any garden supply store and most hardware stores with a gardening section, and the package will contain information about how much to use. Your pH testing kit should also tell you if you need to add any lime and, if so, how much to apply.

Using lime is discussed more thoroughly in Chapter 6.

- Finished compost or garden soil will introduce beneficial bacteria and both are good for getting a new compost pile or bin started.

- Stone dust, which you can obtain from a quarry or land-scape supply store, will add minerals, including calcium and magnesium, that might not otherwise be present that can correct over-acidity in worm bins and kitchen waste systems. A light sprinkling is usually enough to add these valuable minerals to the pile.

WHY ADD STONE DUST TO COMPOST?

At first glance, it may seem odd to add stone dust to compost. After all, the ground contains plenty of stones already. But plants cannot get any nutrients from the rocks their roots encounter. The minerals contained in the rocks are locked together tightly. In order for plants to absorb them, the minerals must be in minute granules that the roots can take up.

Volcanic eruptions regularly bring minerals up from deep in the earth's crust. As volcanic ash breaks down, it releases minerals into the soil that might not be there otherwise. These minerals are an important component in the fertility of soil all over the world. By using stone dust in your compost or limestone on your soil, you are replicating the role of volcanoes by distributing rock dust in tiny granules that plants can use.

Kitchen and household waste

A surprising amount of food waste thrown in the trash every day can be composted. Take breakfast leftovers, for example: coffee grounds and tea leaves, the rind and peels from fruit, and egg

shells can all be added to the compost pile. Coffee and tea are high in nitrogen, and eggshells are mostly calcium, a mineral plants use to build cell walls. The fruit peels provide a high concentration of

A kitchen bowl of vegetable scraps, destined for compost.

carbon, which is essential to plants and a valuable component of compost.

If you plan to compost, one thing you will get used to doing is saving nearly all of your organic kitchen waste. You can use nearly any sort of container for kitchen waste. Garden supply companies (both online and brick-and-mortar stores) sell a wide variety of fancy containers that can match your home décor, but if you are composting to save money and do good for the environment, it does not make sense to buy an item that has to be specially manufactured for a single purpose and then shipped hundreds, or thousands, of miles to get to you. Instead, reuse items such as coffee cans with lids, plastic ice cream or yogurt containers, or a baked bean crock. If you are not familiar with a bean crock, they are large jars made of crockery with tight-fitting lids. This will keep fruit flies out of your scraps and will keep any smells in the crock. If your family eats a lot of fresh fruit and vegetables and produces a lot of waste on a regular basis, you may even want something larger, such as a plastic cat litter bucket or a plastic trash can with a lid.

You can mix household browns, such as torn or shredded paper or the dead leaves from houseplants, with food scraps to help absorb some of the liquid and keep the bin from getting too anaerobic and smelly. You should empty the bin every couple of days, or as it fills, to avoid attracting fruit flies or ants. Always wash the bin with dish detergent and hot water after emptying it. If the container has become infested with mold, as it can during hot weather, you may want to wash it with detergent, and then wash it again with a bit of household bleach in water. Rinse and dry it thoroughly before using it again. You may also want to use biodegradable bags to line the container if you are squeamish about handling the waste.

Food items to compost

You can compost almost any plant-based food item, including fruit and vegetable waste (peels, stems, pulp, and rotted bits); tea leaves and coffee grounds; flour or rice that has gone rancid; and nuts, seeds, and grains. Although these items may no longer be fit for human consumption, the microbes in a compost pile will still break them down into their component parts with no trouble. Any food made mostly from plant matter and raw ingredients that may have spoiled or gone past their prime can be used in composting. Spring cleaning provides an opportunity to clean out the kitchen cupboards and the freezer. Freezer-burned fruit or vegetables can be composted, as can expired yeast, condiments, moldy bread, and stale herbs and spices. While these rancid or freezer-burned foods will not be appetizing to humans, microorganisms will not care that they smell a little bit "off" and will happily consume them.

Large fruit or vegetable seeds, such as peach or avocado pits, will decay, but it may take as long as several months or even years to break down large seeds so you may want to avoid adding them to your compost. Some vegetable seeds may also sprout in the compost pile. If this happens, you can either let them grow or dig them back into the compost to rot. There is a difference of opinion about whether you should eat crops grown in unfinished compost. Some say that to do so can cause stomach upset, while others grow vegetables in their compost on purpose to take advantage of the nutri-

Miscellaneous food items ready for composting.

ents. If you want to beautify your compost pile, you can always allow flowers to grow on it so you get the beauty without the potential of risk to your health.

Eggshells, seashells, and the shells from crustaceans like shrimp and crabs are excellent sources of hard minerals, although they take longer to break down. You should rinse and crush items such as eggshells, seashells, and nutshells so they will break down faster. To crush seashells or crab and lobster shells, rinse and dry them, then put them in a heavy-duty paper bag. Smash the shells with a hammer then pour the contents of the bag into the compost. If you will not be reusing the bag again soon, you can rip it into pieces and compost it. If you are composting salted peanut shells, be sure to thoroughly rinse the salt off them as salt can be bad for a compost pile. Chop up large items, such as whole banana peels, citrus skins, and spoiled fruit and vegetables. Whole citrus peels will decompose more slowly than other fruit peels because they contain antimicrobial oils that can kill off microorganisms in the compost. Cutting them into smaller pieces will help them to break down faster. Too many citrus fruits (such as ones you might get from the local juice shop) might make your compost very acidic. As long as you balance the other ingredients, this should not be a problem, but you will want to test your soil several weeks after using acidic compost on it, just to be sure the pH is in a good range. If you are vermicomposting, go easy on citrus, because it can be harmful to worms.

Non-food items to compost

Many items that are routinely thrown out or recycled can be composted at home. This includes newspaper, paper bags, paper towels used to wipe up food spills, shredded office paper, nonmetallic wrapping paper, cardboard, natural fiber cloth, yarn, or string. Although it is generally better for the environment to recycle these items, you can compost them if you live in an area where you do not have recycling facilities or do not have many deciduous (leaf-bearing) trees, and do not have enough brown materials, such as dead leaves or fallen branches. Shredded paper or cardboard makes good bedding for vermicompost bins, and it absorbs excess fluid in enclosed compost bins and tumblers. You should not try to compost cardboard that is coated in plastic because it will not break down properly, and you may be introducing unwanted chemicals into the compost.

Shredded newspaper ready for composting.

You can dump spent potting soil into the compost after transplanting houseplants to provide some grit for worms and other creatures in the pile and to re-enrich the spent soil. You can also empty the contents of vacuum cleaner bags or canisters into it, as long as you do not have synthetic carpeting. Because synthetic fibers will not break down in compost, it is better not to use vacuum dust if you are not sure what kind of carpeting you have. You can also compost floor sweepings and nail clippings.

Most colored ink is made of vegetable-based dyes now, which makes the inked papers safe to compost. This includes colored newsprint, wrapping paper, and anything with colored ink from a computer printer. Paper takes a very long time to break down, so shred, and dampen the paper before adding it to your compost. Used coffee filters compost well because they are already damp and covered in nitrogen-rich coffee grounds. Glossy paper, like the kind found in magazines and catalogs, will compost eventually, but it can take a long time due to the shiny coating. Because all paper is made of cellulose, it will use up a large amount of nitrogen to break down. The cellulose found in paper and plants provides energy and a source of carbon for the microorganisms in the compost, but it is a good idea to layer paper with fresh grass clippings, coffee grounds, or some other high-nitrogen item to ensure proper and complete composting.

Seaweed is another item you might have on hand if you live anywhere near the ocean. Seaweed contains iodine and boron, which are essential nutrients. Boron helps plants to build cell and seed walls. According to organic lawn care company Ecochem (**www. ecochem.com**), boron is essential for preventing a wide variety of plant disorders, including stunted appearance (rosetting), hollow stems and fruit (hollow heart), and brittle, discolored leaves. Iodine is essential in the human diet, so ensuring that your vegetables have a source of iodine helps make certain that you consume enough iodine to avoid common diseases, such as a goiter, an enlargement of the thyroid gland.

If you collect seaweed from the ocean, do so immediately after a storm or high tide. Do not pick live seaweed as in many areas harvesting seaweed is against the law. Do not pick seaweed that has been sitting on the beach for a long time because it may have a high salt content and will ruin the soil. If the seaweed is dry and crunchy, chances are it

Coastal seaweed ready for collection and composting.

has been there too long. If you pick up seaweed from the beach, choose seaweed that is not rooted in the sand and is still wet and pliable. You can also compost sea grass, but in some areas, it is against the law to collect it. You should call the Department of Natural Resources in your area to make sure it is legal to harvest sea grass if you decide to compost it.

Shells such as egg, crab, shrimp, lobster, clam, mussel, and oyster shells can all be composted. They contain calcium carbonate, which neutralizes acidic soil. Calcium carbonate also prevents a disease called blossom end rot that is caused by calcium deficiency in the soil. This disease causes black spots to appear on the blossom end of fruits such as tomatoes. If you are adding shells from a crustacean to the pile, rinse them well, smash them into small pieces with a hammer, and bury them in the middle of the pile where they will be safe from scavengers. If that is not possible, put them into a digester, tumbler, or other enclosed system to prevent pests from digging them out of the compost.

Natural fibers such as cotton, silk, bamboo, hemp, and wool can be shredded or cut up and added to compost. This is a great way to use up leftover bits of cotton quilting fabric or natural fiber yarns. Because these are all made from natural substances, they will break down easily in the compost. Avoid any cloth that contains any artificial fibers such as polyester, Spandex, or rayon.

If you are doing home renovation and have unpainted scraps of gypsum board or plasterboard, you can smash them up into small pieces and compost them. This product is made from ground gypsum, which is a common mineral, and coated with paper. Modern gypsum board uses recycled paper and low volatile organic compound (VOC) adhesives, so it should not harm your compost if it is used in small amounts. The paper will compost readily, and the gypsum will add minerals to your compost.

Other sources of compost material

If you want to create a large compost heap, but do not have enough material on hand, you may be able to collect it from local businesses that have an excess of leftover organic materials. Here are some suggestions for businesses to approach about collecting compostable materials and the materials you will be able to compost from these businesses.

- Brewery — hops waste (green/nitrogen materials)

- Cider mill — apple waste (green/nitrogen materials)

- Coffee shop — coffee grounds (green/nitrogen materials)

- Farm — manure (green/nitrogen materials) and old hay or straw bales (brown/carbon materials)

- Juice bar — fruit and vegetable pulp and peels (green/nitrogen materials)

- Landscaper — dead leaves, hedge trimmings (brown/carbon materials), and grass clippings (green/nitrogen materials)

- Poultry farm — manure (green/nitrogen materials)

- Quarry — stone dust (marble or granite) (non-organic materials)

- Winery — grape and other fruit waste (green/nitrogen materials)

- Wood shop — untreated sawdust or chips (brown/carbon materials)

Materials to Avoid Composting

Some items just will not compost, and other items contain seeds or chemicals that can invade the garden or damage the soil. You should never introduce anything into your compost that you do not want to spread on your garden. While almost all organic materials can be composted, you should avoid some.

Organic materials

One organic material you should avoid is diseased plants. Diseased plants might break down in the compost, but the composting process may not destroy the pathogen that killed the plant, and it can spread to your other plants. The nutrients you might get out of the diseased plants are not worth the risk of infecting next year's crops, so it is best to dispose of sick plants by whatever method is customary in your area — either by burning them or by disposing of them as directed by your municipal waste authority.

IDENTIFYING DISEASED PLANTS

If a garden plant dies unexpectedly, check to make sure there are no obvious signs of disease before tossing it into the compost pile. Signs of rot, mold, or mildew can indicate any number of plant diseases, and it is probably best not to compost that plant. If a plant dies due to insect infestation, thirst, or some other non-contagious cause, it is perfectly fine to put the plant in the compost. Make sure you rinse away any potentially harmful insects before you add the plant to the compost pile to prevent the possibility of them surviving the composting process and re-infesting your garden.

Plants may have a mineral deficiency rather than a disease. The points below will help you tell if a plant is lacking in nutrients.

- If lower leaves are pale green or yellow or if growth is stunted, the plant may lack magnesium.

- If leaves are red or purple and should not be, the plant may be lacking phosphorus. Plants with this deficiency may also have pale upper leaves and refuse to flower or set fruit.

- If a plant does not seem vigorous and produces small fruit with thin skins, it may be lacking in potassium.

- If lettuce leaves look burnt on the ends, or tomatoes and peppers develop blossom-end rot, the plant lacks calcium.

- If leaves are speckled or curly, if the stem is weak, or the roots are not developing properly, the plant lacks nitrogen or potassium.

- If new leaves are yellowish instead of green, the plant lacks sulphur.

Despite their mineral deficiencies, these plants can be added to the compost if they are disease-free. They will be broken down like any other plant, and the nutrients that they do possess will be passed along to other plants through the process of composting.

Pernicious weeds, especially non-native ones, are extremely hardy, and some of their seeds might survive even in a very hot compost pile. A **pernicious weed** is any weed that is invasive and destructive to other plants or to the habitat it grows in. Often they are non-native species, so the kind of weeds considered pernicious in one area may be tolerated in other states or countries. Some types of pernicious weeds that should not be composted include morning glory, bindweed, sheep sorrel, ivy, several kinds of grasses, and other plants that can regrow from their roots or stems in your compost pile.

Leaf of Platanus with plant disease anthracnose.

To avoid spreading invasive, non-native species, you should burn these plants, if allowed in your area. Other methods of disposal include drowning them for six weeks by weighing them down in a bucket of water, or asphyxiating them by sealing them in a black plastic bag for one year before disposing of them. Otherwise, ask the local waste management authority how to dispose of them. Putting them into a landfill will just allow them to continue spreading, so this may not be the best option.

PUTTING PERNICIOUS WEEDS TO GOOD USE

One good use of pernicious weeds is to make weed tea. Many weeds concentrate minerals and soil nutrients in their taproots, and it is a shame to let those nutrients go to waste. You can make weed tea in much the same way you make compost tea.

1. Secure the weeds in a cloth bag and tie the top tightly so bits of roots or leaves cannot escape.

2. Submerge the bag in a bucket of water and let it soak for at least four to six weeks.

3. After four to six weeks, check the bucket and make sure there is brown sludge in it and that the weeds are dead. This sludge will smell very bad, so you may want to do this in an out-of-the-way place. You can compost the drowned weeds.

4. Dilute the sludge to make a weed tea, one part sludge to ten parts water, and use it to water plants.

Fresh manure, especially chicken manure, is extremely high in nitrogen and can burn plants, causing the leaves and stem to turn brown and wither if it is applied directly to the garden. It is often mixed with urine, which contains urea and exacerbates the problem. Fresh manure contains digestive bacteria that are not helpful to plants and can upset the balance of the compost pile by killing some bacteria. It is best to use aged manure that has been left in the elements for at least six weeks. Horses digest only about one quarter of the grass and grains they eat, which produces weedy manure that may be undesirable for composting. However, cows have four stomachs so their

Cow manure ready for composting.

manure is more digested and has fewer weed seeds in it, making it a better choice for composting. If you cannot obtain manure directly from a farm, you can use bagged manure sold in garden supply stores, but this may be an expensive option. Bagged manure can be used to start a brand new compost pile if you do not already have mature compost to use.

The table shows approximate carbon to nitrogen ratios in the manure of several common animals. Those with higher amounts of carbon will not need as much brown material added along with them. Whatever you have available to you will be helpful to your compost. Just remember to add an appropriate amount of carbon-rich material to offset the high nitrogen content of some manures, especially chicken manure.

| CARBON TO NITROGEN RATIO IN COMMON ANIMAL MANURES ||
TYPE OF MANURE	RATIO
Alpaca, llama, horse, donkey	15:1 to 25:1
Chicken, turkey, rabbit	4:1 (without bedding) 10:1 (with bedding)
Cow, goat, pig, sheep	10:1 to 15:1

You should never use human or pet waste in a conventional compost pile because of the risk of disease, especially worm-borne illnesses. Humans are susceptible to many of the same parasites as dogs and cats, such as hookworms, roundworms, tapeworms, and heartworms. For this reason, handling pet waste is not a good idea. Pregnant women, in particular, as well as people with suppressed immune systems, should not handle cat waste because of the risk of toxoplasmosis, which can cause deafness, blindness, or learning disorders in infants who are infected before birth. Although some high-heat compost systems can destroy pathogens and some advanced gardeners use "humanure," it is best not to take the risk of handling human or pet waste. Horse and cattle manure is different than human or household pet waste because these animals are normally strictly vegetarians and are less likely to pass along diseases. If you do compost dog feces using a commercially produced, pet waste septic system, the resulting compost should never be used on vegetables, herbs, or fruit trees, although it can be used on non-fruit-bearing trees, shrubs, and flowers. A septic system of this kind should be kept away from streams due to the high phosphorous and nitrogen content.

Another organic material you should avoid is coal ash, such as that left over in a charcoal grill. Although charcoal is made from wood, coal ash will introduce sulfur into the compost, and thus into your garden, and will poison the soil. It is best not to use it. You should not put cooked food into compost heaps because it will attract flies and other pests. It can be disposed of in worm bins and digesters. Indoor composting systems can usually handle cooked food, but be sure to follow the guidelines that come with the product.

Items made of real rubber, which is organic, will eventually break down, but it may take several years so rubber should also be avoided. Meat, grease, dairy products, and other animal products, including used cat litter, should not be used in most types of household compost systems. There are three reasons to exclude animal products from your compost.

1. **It will smell.** Decomposing meat will stink unless enclosed in a high-heat compost system designed to break it down.

2. **It may attract vermin.** Rats, raccoons, possums, dogs, and other creatures may come to your compost pile looking for food. These scavengers generally will not be attracted to decomposing plant material, but decomposing meat is what they live on, and if it is in your compost pile, they will be too.

3. **It will slow production of your compost.** Fats found in animal products can coat the vegetable matter and prevent oxygen from reaching the composting material. This will drastically slow the process because the microbes in your compost system need to breathe. If fats and grease smother them, they will die and anaerobic microbes will take over, which will cause an unpleasant odor. The only exception to this is the EM™ Bokashi fermenting compost system, which is designed for anaerobic composting, digester systems, electric composting systems, or worm bins.

Keeping diseased and other compost-unfriendly items out of the compost bin will lead to a healthier garden and a more pleasant composting experience.

Non-organic materials

A compost heap is not a garbage dump. Even though this book started off saying, "garbage becomes a rose," that did not refer to literal garbage. Very few non-organic materials are safe or necessary in a compost heap. You should not try to compost non-organic items, such as glass, metal, cans, bottles, and plastic-coated containers. These should be recycled instead. Plastic-coated containers will not break down properly, and they may introduce undesirable chemicals into your compost, which will then be passed on to your fruit and vegetables. Often, while sifting compost you will find small plastic labels like those found on produce. They will look as shiny and new as they did the day you put them in there because the microbes cannot break down the plastic. Pick them (and any other non-organic items) out of the compost as you sift it.

Items that contain any kind of human waste are not safe for most home composting systems because these systems usually do not get hot enough to kill off the pathogens (viruses and bacteria). These can cause illness when the finished compost is handled. Do not put disposable diapers into compost. Even the ones that are sold as compostable contain human waste, and you should avoid using them in household composting. However, they are safe for use in large municipal composting systems because those systems can compost thousands of pounds of waste at a time, producing extremely hot compost that can kill off nearly all pathogens. Used facial tissues can be composted in hot heaps or totally enclosed systems, but should not be put into the stationary Dalek-type composters because the human pathogens they contain will not break down at cooler temperatures.

Activators

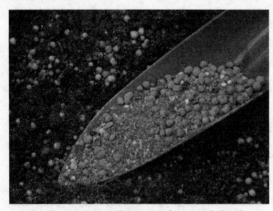

Activators are substances that can help the composting process begin.

Activators are substances that can help the composting process begin, but they are not necessary in most cases. There are many products on the market that claim to help start the composting cycle by introducing beneficial bacteria, enzymes, and hormones. However, because the food and yard waste that is deposited into the compost is already covered in bacteria and because bacteria create their own enzymes to take advantage of their environment, you will not need store-bought activators, or inoculants.

Many activators are designed to introduce more nitrogen into the compost, but adding more fresh green materials will increase the nitrogen enough to start the reaction. The Texas AgriLife Extension Service, which provides information and how-to education on all aspects of agriculture, conducted experiments where compost piles were prepared using a variety of starters, including horse manure, compost, soil, and commercially available activators. Another set of compost piles was prepared using no activators at all. The organization found that there was no major difference between the two groups of compost piles. It concluded that composting would work just as quickly without activators as it will with them; therefore, there is no real benefit to adding bacterial or nitrogen activators to a compost pile. The best way to keep your compost perking away is to keep the correct balance of green and brown items and to aerate it as necessary to allow the microorganisms to do their job.

Some composters like to use activators to get compost going quickly or if they are lacking certain compost ingredients. They are also useful if you do not have finished compost to put into a new pile, although in that case you can just buy a bag of compost and use that to get things started. Composters who live in very cold climates sometimes use activators to make up for the lack of warm temperatures that make bacteria thrive. Most activators contain nitrogen, bacteria, fungi, or some combination. There are both natural and artificial activators, and both types can be found at most gardening supply stores that have a compost section, or online at places such as Amazon (**www.Amazon.com**) or Gardener's Supply Company (**www.gardeners.com**). A quick Internet search will turn up hundreds of places to buy activators, but buying locally may be the best bet if you are not sure exactly what you need, so you can ask a salesperson any questions you may have.

Natural activators

If you are creating compost for organic, chemical-free gardening, you will most likely want to stick to the natural activators, which include compost, soil, manure, and meals of alfalfa, blood, bone, fish, hoof, and horn. **Meals** are created by drying and grinding up organic materials. They can be animal or vegetable in origin. Keep in mind that activators, even the natural ones, and the fruits and vegetables you put in your compost may contain traces of antibiotics, growth hormones, pesticides, and other chemicals.

Alfalfa meal

Alfalfa meal is dried and ground up alfalfa, which is a type of grass high in nitrogen. To use this in your compost, spread a layer every 6 inches in the compost and water well. Alfalfa meal is very useful for heating up a compost pile when you do not have enough green materials to feed it. It contains a small amount of three important nutrients: nitrogen, phosphorous, and potassium. You can purchase a 50-pound bag for about $40.

WHAT IS NPK?

NPK is shorthand for nitrogen, phosphorous, and potassium found in various kinds of fertilizers and soil enhancement products. The initials come from the chemical symbols for each of the nutrients. Nitrogen is N, phosphorous is P, and potassium is K. Each of these nutrients is vital to the health of plants, and you need to be sure that each plant is getting the right amount of each nutrient for that particular plant type.

Fertilizers are labeled with a series of three numbers that indicate the relative amount of nitrogen, phosphorous, and potassium in the given fertilizer. For example, a 5-10-5 fertilizer contains five parts nitrogen, ten parts phosphorous, and five parts potassium.

Blood meal

Blood meal is dried animal blood. It is high in nitrogen and slowly releases it, along with trace minerals, into the compost. (**Trace minerals** are nutrients, such as copper, zinc, and iodine, which are required in the diet in very small or "trace" amounts.) Blood meal is expensive, more than $1 per pound, and is better used directly on the soil around garden plants than directly in the compost. It nourishes the plants and frightens plant-eating animals away. Blood meal is an ingredient in many animal-repelling products. To use blood meal in compost, spread a layer every 6 inches in the compost and water well. To use it on garden plants, mix it with water in the proportions directed on the package.

Bone meal

Bone meal is made of dried, crushed bones. To make your own bone meal, cook bones left over from roasted meats as if you are making stock. Allow the bones to dry out in a low-temperature oven, or put them in the oven after you have used the oven for baking to take advantage of the residual heat. As the bones dry out, crush them in a large mortar and pestle. (A **mortar** is a sturdy container, usually made of stone or wood, in which hard items are ground or pounded into a powder using a **pestle**, a club-shaped stick, usually also made of stone or wood.) Sprinkle the meal onto the compost heap or in the worm bin. Spread a layer every 6 inches in the compost and water well. Bone meal contains a variety of minerals, including calcium, iron, magnesium, phosphorus, and zinc; it makes an excellent bulb fertilizer and can be purchased for just over $1 per pound.

IS IT SAFE TO USE CATTLE-BASED MEALS?

After the mad-cow disease (Bovine spongiform encephalopathy) scare in the 1990s, the U.S. Food and Drug Administration (FDA) made changes in how commercially raised cattle are fed in the United States. According to the FDA, these changes, made in 1997, forbid the use of mammal protein, such as beef or mutton in the feed given to ruminants. Therefore, it is considered safe to use products such as blood meal, bone meal, and hoof and horn meal manufactured since that time.

Even though cattle-based meals have been declared safe, blood, hoof, bone, and horn meal are all by-products of cattle processing, and some people choose not to use them. For the same reason, some people choose not to use feather meal, which is a by-product of chicken processing. There are a variety of non-animal-based meals to choose from that will do the job just as well.

Compost

Using compost from a previous batch is a good way to introduce beneficial bacteria and enzymes to a new compost pile. Spread a 2-inch layer of finished compost every 12 inches when layering materials.

Cottonseed meal

Cottonseed meal is made of dried and ground-up cotton seeds. Cotton is a heavily sprayed crop and the cottonseed meal may contain pesticides, so it is best to avoid it if you are trying to make organic compost or if you intend to use the compost on food plants. To use cottonseed meal, spread a layer every 6 inches in the compost and water well. Cottonseed meal is high in nitrogen and also contains phosphorus, potash, and other minor elements. Cottonseed meal can acidify the soil. According to organic garden supply company Extremely Green (**www.extremelygreen. com**), it takes 9 pounds of limestone to neutralize the acidity of 100 pounds of cottonseed meal, so consider this when using it. Cottonseed meal costs about $1 per pound.

Feather meal

Feather meal is made from cooked, dried, pulverized chicken feathers. It has an NPK content of 13-0-0, so has the same nitrogen content as blood meal. It degrades over the course of two or three months, more slowly than blood meal. It is good for mixing with mature compost as a fertilizer. Feather meal will not heat up a compost pile. It costs just over $1 per pound.

Fish meal

Fish meal is dried and ground-up fish or fish parts. The oil and water is pressed out of the fish, and the remaining product is dried. Spread a layer every 6 inches in the compost and water well. Fish meal is high in nitrogen, amino acids, and vitamins. It has an NPK content of 10-6-2 and releases these nutrients quickly at temperatures above 60 degrees. The strong odor may attract animals, so keep that in mind when using fish meal on your compost. It costs just under $1 per pound.

Hoof meal and horn meal

Hoof meal is made from the ground-up hooves of ruminant animals, while horn meal is made from their horns. The raw material is obtained from slaughterhouses and cattle processors. Both are high in nitrogen and have some phosphorus. The nutrients leach more slowly from hoof and horn meal than they do from blood meal, giving plants a more constant source of nutrition. Spread a layer every 6 inches in the compost and water well.

Manure

You can use dry, aged manure from poultry, including chickens, geese, ducks, turkeys, and pigeons. You can also use horse, cow, sheep, goat, llama, or pig manure, and manure from small animals like rabbits. Aged manure is best for composting, as fresh manure is often wet and introduces too much moisture to the compost. Manure contains nitrogen, phosphorus, potassium, and minor nutrients such as calcium, magnesium, and sulfur.

Soil

Garden soil from a healthy patch of ground is rich in microorganisms and macro organisms. Avoid using soil from areas that have been sprayed with herbicides or pesticides because they linger in the soil. Use about 2 inches of soil for every 6 inches of other materials.

Urine

Urine contains urea, which is high in nitrogen. If you are using manure in your compost, chances are it already contains urine. Some composters dilute their own urine (four parts urine to one part water) and pour it on the compost pile instead of plain water. Urine is also a bacterial activator and is useful if you do not have mature compost to add to the bin.

Bacterial activators are useful in very hot, dry, or cold environments where bacteria grow slowly. They cannot hurt the compost, but studies show that they will not help it much either. Whether you use them or not is up to you. Some composters report better outcomes when using activators, although studies by the Texas Agrilife Extension Service (see below) have shown that they make no difference to the outcome.

All these activators are high in either nitrogen or bacteria. Vegetarians and vegans may want to avoid using blood, bone, fish, hoof or horn meal, and possibly manure, but alfalfa and cottonseed meal, compost, and soil are all non-animal sources of natural activators.

DOG FOOD IN MY COMPOST?

Dog food, as well as rabbit, chicken, or goat feed, can act as natural nutritional activators in compost by providing a large hit of nitrogen. For example, 15 pounds of rabbit or goat feed will heat a cubic yard of compost to about 140 degrees. Check the label to make sure it is a 100 percent vegetable formula.

Animal feeds typically heat the pile quickly and are consumed quickly, so it is helpful to add another, longer-lasting source of nitrogen to the pile when you add the feed. You can use manure or fresh grass clippings in conjunction with the feed to maintain heat in the pile beyond the initial burst of energy.

To heat up the average-sized home compost heap, which is about 12 cubic feet, or slightly less than a cubic yard, add about 20 percent grass clippings or manure (1 part grass or manure to 4 parts compost) and one of the following:

- 8 pounds of cottonseed meal

- 20 pounds of dog food, or rabbit or poultry feed

- 10 pounds of soybean meal or canola meal

- 8 pounds of organic fertilizer

A pile heated this way should be turned every two days and watered as needed until it cools.

Artificial activators

The most common artificial compost activators are chemical fertilizers. These products give compost a big surge of heat by adding nitrogen, and if there is not enough carbon-rich material to counteract it, your compost can burn too hot and turn anaerobic once all the carbon has been used up. Make sure to keep the balance of green and brown in mind when using artificial activators.

Chemical fertilizer

You can use a 10-5-10 fertilizer, which provides 10 percent nitrogen, 5 percent phosphorus, and 10 percent potassium, to spike a compost pile. Every fertilizer should list what ratio of nutrients it provides on the package. This will help you choose the right fertilizer for your needs. If you choose to use fertilizer, you should use 1 cup of fertilizer for every 10 square feet of level compost pile surface and repeat this every 6 inches. However, chemical fertilizers do not have protein mixed with their nitrogen the way natural activators do and are not as helpful to compost.

Ammonium sulfate is a type of manufactured fertilizer that combines nitrogen and sulfur. It can be diluted with water and is sprayed on croplands. While adding this product to your compost bin or pile will introduce a large amount of nitrogen, it will defeat one of the main purposes of making compost in the first place: to have a free form of fertilizer that is completely organic or at least mostly free of chemicals. If you are going to buy ammonium sulfate to feed your soil, you will be better off spraying it directly onto your garden rather than putting it in your compost. Be aware that the state of California requires a warning on this product because it is known to cause cancer, birth defects, or other reproductive harm. While it is used on many commercial crops, you should carefully consider adding this chemical to your vegetables or herbs. This product has also been shown to acidify the soil and harm some species of earthworms.

Ammonium nitrate is another common fertilizer that is sometimes recommended for composting. It will not heat a compost heap very much, and it may kill the microorganisms in the compost. Be aware that in the United States there are both federal and state laws concerning how much ammonium nitrate a person can buy at one time because people have used this product to make bombs. Other countries may have similar laws.

Preparing Waste for Composting

Collecting your kitchen and yard waste is only part of the process. Whole fruits and vegetables, entire branches, and bundles of paper will not compost very well if left in that state. The smaller the materials are, the easier it will be for the organisms in the compost to consume them. On the other hand, you do not want to reduce materials to a powder because they can compact and reduce airflow, therefore slowing decomposition. Heavy vines, like those from pumpkins or tomatoes, should be chopped up, and items like branches and corncobs can be crushed with a hammer. You should pierce the skins of whole fruits and vegetables or chop up large pieces of fruit so that bacteria can get inside more quickly.

You should process branches and sticks with a wood chipper; shred leaves; chop food waste into small pieces; and crush items like egg or seashells. To speed the process of composting, you should tear up paper and cardboard and soak it in water for a few minutes before adding it to the compost bin or pile. To compost cardboard boxes, remove all tape, stickers, and staples and soak the cardboard in water for at least ten minutes. The water will leach out water-soluble glue and other chemicals. Pour this water in a place where edible plants cannot absorb it. The small amount of glue residue left on the cardboard will not harm the compost because the fungi and microorganisms will decompose it.

Composting weeds

As mentioned earlier, some weeds contain a wealth of nutrients that they pull up via their deep root system. These weeds can be used in composting, but to prevent propagating the weeds, you should take some precautions. Some weeds can go to seed even after they are pulled from the ground, so to prevent this, let them dry in the sun for three to four days. After they have dried, put them into a hot compost pile (at least 135 degrees) and let them cook at that temperature for several days to kill off the seeds and roots.

The following table compares the various types of compost systems, and lists some of the pros and cons of each type.

Type	Pros	Cons
Pile or heap (slow/warm or cool)	Easy to use. Little effort to maintain. Can add ingredients as they are accumulated.	Takes a year or more to make compost. May smell. May leach nutrients.
Pile or heap (fast/hot)	Makes compost quickly. Kills weeds and some pathogens. Nutrients leached more slowly.	Requires a large amount of material in the beginning. Takes a lot of effort to turn and maintain the pile.
Stationary box	Looks tidy (good for urban areas). Produces compost relatively quickly if well maintained.	Box must be built or purchased. May be hard to turn contents.
Tumbler	Easy to use and aerate. No leaching of nutrients.	May be expensive to buy. Works best if you fill it all at once.
Pit or trench	Relatively simple to do. No building or purchase necessary as long as you have a shovel.	Only nourishes a small patch of land. Does not store much waste.
Sheet	Good for large areas. Consumes a lot of material. No purchase or building necessary.	Requires effort to plant the crop then to till or turn material into the soil. Takes up to a season to decompose.
Trash bag	Inexpensive and easy to do. Can be done year-round and indoors.	Anaerobic process will smell bad. May attract pests.
Vermicomposting	Easy to do. Uses food waste continuously. No smell.	Requires some investment to build or buy a worm bin. Need to ensure worms are properly fed and kept at the right temperature.

In the next chapter, you will explore the science behind composting. What actually happens in the compost pile to turn scraps into compost? How do bacteria and insects contribute to the process? How can you speed up composting or slow it down?

CASE STUDY

Kimberly Wolterman,
co-owner and vice president
Organic Resource Management, Inc.
13060 County Park Road,
Florissant, MO 63034
www.ormiorganics.com
composthappens@sbcglobal.net

"I am co-owner of a commercial composting business and also compost at home. Because we own a commercial composting facility, we can easily dispose of the leaves generated by our numerous trees and obtain finished compost whenever we need it.

We also keep a compost bin in the backyard. It is a simple, chicken-wire bin, but it gives us a place to recycle trimmings off plants and other yard waste. It is a slower process of decomposition, but it ultimately gets the job done, proving that you do not have to pay a lot of money for a composting system.

Why should we care about composting? In the United States, 12 percent of the landfill space is taken up by yard waste and 11 percent by food waste.

We have had a vermicompost bin in our house for the past ten years. We initially started a bin because we go to schools and give presentations on composting, and the worms provide a great visual of the composting process. Plus, the kids love the worms. When I take our worm bin into classrooms, I always allow time for the children to feel the compost and look closely at the worms. My favorite moment is when they realize what they have their hands in, and go, 'Ewwwww, worm poop!'

Both of our own children used the worm bin in science fair projects, and this year my great niece used it as well. From a recycling standpoint, it is amazing how much food waste the worms can consume. This prevents it from being placed in the landfill or sent down the garbage disposal. We use the worm castings to enrich the soil of our potted plants and collect the excess liquid from the worm bin to use as compost tea for the plants.

Composting is pretty much a no-brainer. It is the right thing to do for the environment; it does not require that much work; and you get a beautiful product that enhances your garden for free. It means a lot to me to know that I am keeping a valuable resource out of the landfill while at the same time being able to produce a product that enhances my plants and my gardens. We use compost in all of our planting beds and in all our pots containing vegetables, herbs, and annuals. Every time we cut in a new bed, we enrich the soil with compost prior to planting.

Composting happens every day in nature. Anyone can set up a compost bin, because it is a very basic process. You can simply toss grass clippings, leaves, and other yard debris in a heap and let nature do the rest, or you can set up a more sophisticated system to speed the process along. Either way, you can help the environment and your gardens at the same time. For me, the most difficult part for composting is turning the compost pile, which can be a challenge when using the single bin, chicken-wire system.

Why should we care about composting? In the United States, 12 percent of the landfill space is taken up by yard waste and 11 percent by food waste. By doing our part in recycling our own yard trimmings and food waste, we can save landfill space and help reduce methane production in landfills. All that, and you end up with a beautiful product that will improve your soil structure by adding organic matter. What's not to love?"

CHAPTER 3

THE SCIENCE OF COMPOSTING

"All this new stuff goes on top / turn it over, turn it over / wait and water down / from the dark bottom / turn it inside out / let it spread through / Sift down even. / Watch it sprout. / A mind like compost."

— Gary Snyder, poet

The science behind composting is simple: fungi and microorganisms in the soil break down organic materials into their basic components, making those basic components available to the root systems of living plants. Think of a forest floor. The leaves and other debris from trees, plants, and animals are continually broken down by natural processes and become food for the next generation of trees and plants. A single teaspoon of healthy soil contains billions of microorganisms, but the natural composting process is still slow in nature. Composting can speed this natural process up dramatically because it concentrates compost materials in a contained space, with the number of bacteria in a healthy compost heap doubling every hour.

This large population of microorganisms heats up the contents of the compost and assists in decomposing the materials and killing any pathogens.

Composting relies on five main ingredients: air, water, carbon, nitrogen, and small organisms. If any one of these ingredients is not present, then composting will not take place, or it will take place at such a slow rate that it will do you no good as a gardener. If you supply the first four ingredients, the organisms will do their part, and in just a few months, you will have rich compost.

Essential Composting Elements

There are two ways items in compost can break down: aerobic and anaerobic decomposition. **Aerobic composting** requires oxygen, moisture, carbon, and nitrogen, and it is most efficient when all these things are present in the correct amounts. **Anaerobic composting** does not require much, if any, oxygen, but also will not provide all the benefits of aerobic composting. Both kinds of composting are achieved through the actions of microorganisms, but the kinds of bacteria and fungi that live in an aerobic compost are different than those in an anaerobic pile. Aerobic composting has air-breathing microorganisms that will warm the pile as they work. The gases they release have no odor. Anaerobic composting has non-air-breathing microorganisms that release toxic, odorous gases into the atmosphere. It is much more pleasant to be around an aerobic compost bin than an anaerobic one.

Oxygen

The aerobic microorganisms that decompose organic waste require oxygen. Turning or mixing the compost when the temperature is right, will aerate the materials, introducing enough oxygen to keep the microbes alive and active. Some types of compost systems have air holes in the container or raise the compost pile off the ground to allow for better airflow. Keeping a constant level of oxygen is important. The oxygen level should be kept at a minimum of 5 percent according to the Texas AgriLife Extension Service, but a higher percentage of oxygen will speed up decomposition and will significantly decrease the problem of offensive odors. It is not practical to measure the oxygen level in your home compost pile, but if you turn the pile each time it starts to cool, there should be adequate oxygen to keep things cooking.

Air will penetrate about 18 to 24 inches into the pile from all directions so the widest you should make the pile is 4 feet. This should allow adequate air penetration. You should put layers of coarse material, such as small branches, throughout the pile to facilitate air infiltration. You can also use large PVC pipes with holes drilled in them to allow air into the pile. These pipes can stick out of the top or sides of the pile. A pile that is 4 to 6 feet tall will compost more quickly than a smaller pile as the mass of materials helps keep the pile warm and provides more food for the microorganisms. A pile that is 3-by-3 feet will be easier for most people to turn, but a larger pile will get hotter and, therefore, will be more efficient, so take this into account when setting up your compost. While a large pile may be better in some respects, it will not be any good at all if you cannot physically maintain it. As a pile cooks, it will shrink from 20 percent to 60 percent, depending on the materials used to build it, so do not be disappointed when you see that your pile of compost is significantly smaller than the pile of waste that you started out with. The nutrients in it are just more compact, concentrated, and better for your garden than a random pile of scraps would be.

If you are using an enclosed stationary compost bin, you will have to aerate the compost by another means because air cannot penetrate as well through the normally small holes found in plastic bins.

Aerobic Decomposition

Aerobic composting uses oxygen. The respiration of the microbes makes the compost warm up, helping to kill off weed seeds and plant diseases. Extremely hot compost piles, or so-called hot heaps, if maintained at the right level, can destroy weed seeds, human and animal pathogens, and parasites, such as round worms that are common in animal waste, resulting in healthier soil. This level of heat is difficult to maintain in most small, home-based systems. If you do maintain a hot heap, it is important not to let the compost get too hot, or the decomposition process can slow or stop.

WHAT IS A HOT HEAP?

Some composters enjoy the challenge of building a compost heap that cooks at very high temperatures, up to 150 degrees or hotter. This kind of heap eats up a lot of material very quickly and requires dedication and a strong back (or heavy machinery). The materials in a hot heap are identical to the materials in an ordinary compost heap. The difference lies in how they are handled. You must turn hot heaps regularly before they start to cool down. *Chapter 4 has instructions for building a hot heap.*

Anaerobic Decomposition

In an unhealthy compost pile, anaerobic, or non-oxygen using, microorganisms can multiply, causing a host of problems. Instead of moist, porous soil, you will end up with sticky, rotting muck. This happens because as these organisms consume the compost material, they cause the materials to ferment and leave behind organic acids, ammonia, and methane as by-products. These gases cause an unhealthy compost pile to smell bad. You can avoid this by turning or aerating the compost pile regularly when it reaches a given temperature and by carefully balancing the kinds of materials you put into the compost. If the compost gets too wet, you should stir or turn it daily and put in dry materials such as leaves or shredded paper or cardboard. These materials will soak up the water and provide additional carbon to balance out the nitrogen-containing green materials.

In some cases, you might want to create anaerobic compost if you will be away from home for an extended period and will not be able to tend to your compost pile. You may also want this if you use methods of anaerobic composting, such as trash bag composting and indoor composting with products like the EM™ Bokashi system. An outdoor pile that is left to cool off after the first wave of hot aerobic microbes die off will become anaerobic on its own. The anaerobic bacteria will move in to take over where the aerobic ones left off. They have slower metabolisms and will compost much more slowly. If you want to revert to aerobic composting, add more carbon-rich materials and turn or stir the compost. In a matter of days, the aerobic microbes will have taken over once again.

Moisture

Water is another vital component of a healthy compost system because the microbes are living organisms and require water to live. If the system is enclosed, or you live in a dry climate, you will have to water it periodically. The compost should not be soggy, because too much water will cause the compost pile to turn mushy and will create a foul smell as the anaerobic microbes take over. If compost becomes saturated, turn it to help it dry out, and the composting process should start up again. You should aim for moisture content of 45 percent to 50 percent. When you squeeze a handful of compost, almost no water — a few drops at most — should come out. You can water the compost with plain water from a garden hose, even if it is chlorinated. You can also use the water from cooked vegetables, provided there is no butter, oil, or other grease mixed in. Vegetable water contains minerals and nutrients that were cooked out of the vegetables, making it beneficial to include in the compost. Do not use dishwater on the compost pile because it will contain grease and detergent.

Carbon

A healthy aerobic compost system should contain a carbon to nitrogen ratio of about 25 or 30 parts to one. Carbon, or brown material, is vital to the compost because the microorganisms that live in the compost system use it for energy and for building and maintaining their own bodies. These microorganisms ingest carbon and exhale carbon dioxide so they need a constant supply of carbon-containing materials. However, too much carbon in the compost can slow decomposition to almost nothing.

Nitrogen

A source of nitrogen is essential for composting to work, because nitrogen provides energy to the microorganisms that consume the compost materials. Nitrogen exists in all living, or recently living, plants and animals. You can find nitrogen in items such as kitchen waste, fresh grass clippings, nearly any wet or green organic material, and in the various types of meal (for example, blood meal or fish meal) made from animals. An excess of nitrogen in the compost will cause aerobic bacteria to eat up all the carbon very quickly, and the bacteria will then die off if you do not add more carbon-rich materials. The absence of bacteria will cause anaerobic microbes to thrive, and they will release ammonia gas, which is a sign of a poorly maintained aerobic compost system. Too much nitrogen will also increase your compost's pH level, which can kill some microorganisms. However, too little nitrogen will mean that your pile composts very slowly.

Most materials contain a mixture of carbon and nitrogen. Some green materials contain more carbon than others as shown in the following table from the University of Illinois Extension. The University of Illinois Extension, which is affiliated with the University of Illinois at Urbana-Champaign, offers education to all of Illinois residents. Their website contains a wealth of information on gardening, composting, and other agricultural and horticultural topics. The table gives approximate carbon and nitrogen amounts for various kinds of yard and kitchen waste starting with those that are highest in carbon. If you are using materials that are very high in carbon, make sure to mix them with materials that are high in nitrogen so you can maintain an approximate 25 to 1 or 30 to 1 ratio. You can see from this table that green hay and weeds both have a 25 to 1 ratio of carbon to nitrogen, which means they are almost perfect for composting because they usually contain exactly the right ratio. There will be individual differences in any given pile of hay or weeds, but, in general, they are very close to the ideal ratio. You can pile them up and let them compost on their own, and the pile will work very efficiently. However, wood chips, which have a 500 to 1 carbon to nitrogen ratio, will require a large amount of green materials along with them to put them into balance.

Material	Carbon: Nitrogen Ratio
Wood chips	500-700:1
Sawdust	200-500:1
Paper	170-200:1

Material	Carbon: Nitrogen Ratio
Leaves, pine	60-100:1
Corn stalks	50-100:1
Straw	40-100:2
Leaves, other	30-80:1
Fruit waste	35:1
Hay, green	25:1
Weeds	25:1
Leaves, ash, black elder, and elm	21-28:1
Manure, horse and cow	20-25:1
Seaweed	19:1
Grass clippings	12-25:1
Vegetable waste	12-25:1

Organisms

Several organisms are responsible for breaking down the materials in a compost system, but perhaps the most important are bacteria, fungi, and molds. These organisms are present on all compost materials in some amount, and they flourish or decline based on the environment they find themselves in and how much food is available to them. They work together, each at a different point of decomposition, to decay the various materials in the compost system. In addition to the microorganisms, larger creatures, such as insects, mollusks, and worms, all contribute to decomposing the compost ingredients. As a compost pile cools, it can also attract other creatures, such as toads, frogs, birds, and bats. These creatures are harmless and will hunt the insects that live in the pile to take advantage of the pile's warmth and dampness. Their presence is an indication of a healthy, diverse, compost pile.

You may wonder why it matters what organisms live in the compost and what they do, but this knowledge can help you create a more efficient composting environment. For example, if you have a lot of paper products or fibrous plants that are very high in cellulose, it is helpful to know that they will remain more or less intact through the high-temperature period of composting and not be broken down until the end when the pile cools and certain organisms take over. Below is a brief overview of the various kinds of microorganisms that help break down the materials in compost.

Microorganisms

Microorganisms are responsible for warming the compost pile. As they consume the materials and respire, they release heat. At the start of composting when the mass of materials is cool, pyschrophilic bacteria flourish. They can live in temperatures between 0 and 65 degrees. At slightly higher temperatures (70 to 90 degrees), mesophilic or low-temperature bacteria flourish. As the temperature in the compost increases past 100 degrees, thermophilic or high-temperature bacteria begin to predominate. These are thought to be primarily responsible for decomposing protein and organic matter, and they survive in the compost even at very high temperatures.

The temperature of a newly created compost pile will remain high for about three to five days unless you keep feeding and turning it, in which case it will remain hot for as long as you tend it. A hot compost pile will kill more pathogens, weed seeds, and roots, so it is advantageous to keep the pile hot for as long as possible. Bacteria can die if the temperature of the compost suddenly drops or if the environment becomes too acidic, so it is important to keep the pile warm and to ensure the proper balance of nutrients to keep the bacteria healthy. You want the bacteria to thrive because the composting process will slow down if the bacteria die. Organisms such as fungi and **actinomycetes**, which are bacteria that resemble fungi, are present throughout the composting process, but take over near the end of the cycle as the compost is cooling down to decompose cellulose, lignin, and other difficult-to-decay materials. Cellulose and lignin are the materials that make up the walls of cells. They are especially tough in paper and cardboard because these items are made from wood. Fungi and actinomycetes seem to have the greatest success processing paper and similar items, even though many other kinds of bacteria can also consume cellulose.

- Fungi are primitive plants, such as mushrooms, that lack chlorophyll. These organisms thrive by consuming the remains of dead plants and animals. Most fungi flourish in a compost system when the temperature is a relatively cool 70 to 75 degrees, and they do their work near the end of the composting cycle, although some can survive in temperatures up to 120 degrees.

- Actinomycetes work below the surface of the earth to convert dead organic material into a substance similar to peat, a porous, decayed, organic matter that accumulates in wetlands. These actinomycetes release carbon, nitrogen, and ammonia, making it available to plants. These organisms, which thrive between 50 and 115 degrees, are responsible for the fresh smell of good, clean soil and make a natural antibiotic substance that kills off bacteria. They will form a gray or white web in the compost that may look like mold.

Macro organisms

Larger organisms, such as mites, beetles, flies, millipedes, centipedes, slugs, snails, ants, and worms, decompose compost materials by biting, tearing, grinding, sucking, or chewing them, making the materials smaller and more usable to the chemical decomposers. They thrive at temperatures below 80 degrees and will not always be present in a compost system.

Some organisms help the composting process by introducing or moving bacteria, fungi, and minerals. Ants move materials around and can bring fungi (which they eat) into the compost along with minerals like phosphorus and potassium. Flies carry bacteria to the compost pile on their feet, and this can benefit the compost; however, a breeding population of flies on a compost pile can quickly become a problem.

In vermicomposting, worms are the primary method of composting, but even in a regular compost system, worms can play an important role as long as they can get into the compost pile. They will thrive in an outdoor pile that touches the soil. Obviously there will be no worms in an enclosed system, and you should not put worms into such a system because the high temperatures will kill them. The exception to this is a vermicompost bin that is designed specifically for worms. Many types of worms, including microscopic nematodes and flat worms, are found in the average compost pile. Earthworms are the most useful creatures when it comes to making soil fertile because they continuously digest soil and organic matter, grinding and fermenting it before excreting it as castings. Fresh earthworm castings contain more organic material — nitrogen, calcium, magnesium, phosphorus, and potassium — than soil itself, according to Texas Agrilife Extension Service.

The Chemical Process of Decomposition

Organic materials consist of carbon and nitrogen in differing amounts. In an aerobic composting environment, organisms essentially eat the compost materials. They consume nitrogen, phosphorus, and carbon along with other nutrients such as potash, also called potassium carbonate. Potash is a compound found in wood ashes, and it can supply necessary potassium to crops. The organisms in the compost use the carbon for energy and release carbon dioxide as a by-product of their respiration. They also store some carbon in their cells and need higher levels of carbon than nitrogen in the compost. Too much carbon can reduce their efficiency, and it will take longer for the materials to break down. Maintaining a proper balance of green and brown compost ingredients will lead to faster creation of compost. To ensure a healthy balance of carbon to nitrogen, you can weigh materials and put in 1 pound of nitrogen or green material for every 25 to 30 pounds of carbon-rich or brown materials, or just estimate. If the balance is off slightly, it will not harm the compost pile, and it is easy to amend the pile by adding more of one or the other. If you have a smaller compost system, such as an indoor container, reduce the amount of each material by half or one quarter, whatever is necessary to fill your container. If reducing the quantity by half, you will use ½ pound of green material with 12 ½ to 15 pounds of brown material. If you are reducing the quantity by one quarter, you will use ¼ pound of green material with 6 ¼ to 7 ½ pounds of brown material, and so on.

Do not let the measurements and ratios worry you. Compost is more like making soup than baking a cake. Baking is a science where measurements must be exact and straying from the directions can ruin the outcome. You mix up the batter and pop it in the oven, hoping that a delicious, evenly risen cake will result, but if you tinker with the recipe you will not really know what the final cake will look or taste like until after it has baked. Making soup is more of a trial-and-error process. You start with the basic ingredients, add a little of this, a little of that, and sample it as you go to see how it is doing and what else it might need.

Compost is very much like that, although the sampling is done visually and by smell. If the pile is too cool and not decomposing, add green items. If it is too hot or wet, add brown ones. If it smells bad, it is probably too wet or anaerobic. If it smells like fresh clean dirt, it is probably almost ready to use. Small adjustments can be made as needed to get the outcome you desire.

You must protect the compost system from extreme heat and cold and from very wet or dry conditions so that the microorganisms can do their job. If you are in a cold area, it is wise to insulate the pile using an old carpet or blanket. You may also want to situate the compost bin so that the open side faces south to take advantage of the sunlight. If you are in a wet area, or your compost system does not have a lid, make sure there is adequate drainage and that you have something to cover the pile. A plastic tarp is all right as long as it does not touch the pile and prevents oxygen infiltration. You can cover the pile during heavy rains as long as you remember to remove the tarp later.

To keep an open compost pile or heap properly insulated, it should be at least 3 feet by 3 feet. This size will stay warm and moist and be manageable enough to turn with a pitchfork. Smaller piles will work, but will mature more slowly. If you live in a cool or windy area, or want to maintain a hotter compost heap, you may want to build a larger pile — at least 4 feet by 4 feet and 5 or 6 feet high — to maintain the proper level of heat. Without the heat aerobic organisms produce, the compost will decompose very slowly, and if anaerobic organisms take over, the compost pile will begin to stink as the composting process slows down. It will eventually be usable, but most homeowners will not want the smell of a rotting compost pile near their home.

Slow compost systems

A slow compost heap is one with a large percentage of carbon — perhaps a ratio of 200:1 or higher — in it. It can take up to two years for a slow compost pile to generate usable compost, but this system may be preferable if you do not have the strength to turn a compost pile very often, or if you are just looking for a way to use up waste material and do not need the compost quickly. This type of heap does not have to be turned as often or at all, making it a very easy kind of compost pile to keep, but if you want to maintain the oxygen level, you should turn the pile about once every month or two in order to encourage aerobic bacteria to thrive. It will still make usable compost, but because it will not get hot, you should never put diseased plants or any animal products into the pile because they will not fully break down, and you will run the risk of spreading disease to your other plants. You can put raw food products, such as fruits and vegetables, into a slow compost system, but you should avoid using any cooked food, meat, bones, fat, or dairy.

Medium compost systems

If you do not have a lot of time to devote to composting, or do not have enough material on hand to create a large, hot heap, you can still create compost within three to nine months. A carbon to nitrogen ratio of about 40:1 to 200:1 will help maintain a medium compost heap, so you will need to stock up on brown, carbon-rich materials, such as old leaves, shredded paper or cardboard, and brown trimmings from the garden. A compost heap smaller than 3 feet by 3 feet or one that is turned no more than once a month will compost, but it will break down at a slower rate, and it will not be as efficient at killing off pathogens, weed seeds, and plant diseases. This is often the best type of compost pile for a casual gardener who does not have much time or energy to tend to a faster, hotter compost pile.

Fast compost systems

You can make fast compost in two to three weeks if the ratio of carbon to nitrogen is correct and if you turn the pile religiously every three days. Fast compost requires a low carbon to nitrogen ratio ranging from 20:1 to 40:1. Your exact ratio will depend on what materials you have on hand and how many of each you have, but try to shoot for this range. You may notice that this ratio is in the same neighborhood as that recommended for any kind of aerobic composting. This gives the microorganisms lots of carbon to eat and enough nitrogen to give them energy. What makes this pile faster and hotter than a standard compost pile is when and how often you turn it. Turning the pile every three days before it has a chance to cool down will introduce more carbon into the center of the pile to feed the microorganisms. This keeps them alive and reproducing longer, and the more of them there are, the hotter the pile will get.

The microorganisms' respiration releases a lot of heat, and it is best not to let your compost get hotter than 155 degrees because the azobacteria that convert nitrogen gas into a plant-soluble form will die around 160 degrees. If your compost pile does get above 155 degrees, take the pile apart and rebuild it to cool it down. Azobacteria live in soil and make nitrate nitrogen, which is required in large quantities for vegetables, especially corn that needs between 120 and 160 pounds of nitrates per acre. These bacteria consume humus and require a balance of minerals, including calcium. They thrive at a pH level between 5.75 and 7.25.

Well-maintained home systems can reach about 150 degrees in about three days, and when the pile starts to cool off you should turn it so that material on the outside is brought to the inside where it can compost. If you do this every three days, you will maintain very hot compost that will kill off harmful bacteria and the eggs of many parasites that may be present in the compost ingredients. Frequent turning and a carbon to nitrogen ratio of about 20:1 or 40:1 will help maintain a fast, hot heap. *Instructions for creating a hot heap are included in Chapter 4.*

No matter what type of compost you choose to make, the final product will be the same. It may just take varying amounts of time and effort to get to that end product. Whether you invest the time and energy to make fast compost or take the more leisurely route of just piling the ingredients up and letting them do their own thing, you will end up with beautiful black gold — compost.

CASE STUDY
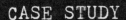

Andrea Zuercher
Amateur composter
Lawrence, Kansas

"I use compost to add organic matter to the soil throughout my garden, in both the ornamental and vegetable sections. Adding organic matter is one of the best ways to improve the heavy clay soil we have here in northeast Kansas. I am a casual or a 'slow' composter. I do not focus on the proper ratio of green to brown for optimal compost making. I see it as a way to use vegetable and fruit matter from my kitchen, keeping it out of the landfills, and I eventually end up with compost that I can use to improve my soil. Composting might seem like hard work, but it does not have to be. If you are not in a hurry for your compost, you can avoid having to be precise about ratios of green to brown.

The previous owner of my house had started a compost pile made of wooden pallets. I used that until an excavation project meant that it had to go. I then bought a black plastic compost bin and have used it ever since. It is not very large, and I have never relied solely on it for the compost I need for my garden (getting the rest of the compost from the city compost program). However, it has produced quite a few batches of usable compost over the years.

I save kitchen scraps and trimmings from my perennial gardens and shrubs. The bulk of our yard waste goes into big paper bags and gets picked up by the city once a week during the growing season. The city has a composting program through which residents can buy compost in the spring and fall. By contributing to the city composting, I can avoid having to compost large or woody debris, which will not break down very quickly in my small composter. Yet the organic materials do not go to waste and do not end up in the landfills.

Composting is not difficult, but there are some unpleasant aspects to it. In the grand scheme of things, it is not that hard to collect kitchen scraps, but it is sometimes a pain to do it, especially in the winter. Sometimes my small collection bin gets smelly and yucky, with fly and fruit fly larvae all over it. Sometimes it attracts fruit flies, which then inhabit my kitchen. I wish I had a better way of collecting compostables with an integrated bin in my kitchen that would not get smelly. My boyfriend, who shares my house with me, is not fond of having kitchen scraps collecting even for a little while on top of the counter, which I sometimes do if I do not feel like trekking out to the bin with only a handful of lettuce or a banana peel. I do not do indoor composting because I live in a house where I can compost outside.

I would prefer a two- or three-compartment open system that will allow me to turn the compost by moving it from bin to bin. The black bin does not allow for this kind of turning. However, it does help keep critters away, which is important in an urban setting. Several times I have left compostable items (mostly fruit and veggie scraps) on my back porch because I did not feel like trekking out to the bin by the garage, and have come out in the morning to find the scraps strewn around the porch by a critter (usually a possum). In the closed bin, they cannot get to it, and so they do not hang out in my yard.

My parents, who have a large, somewhat woody, compost pile have had several 'surprises' grow up out of their compost, such as an amaryllis (whose bulb was given up as spent, but that apparently just needed the supportive conditions of a compost pile), which emerged and bloomed beautifully in the middle of the summer.

One time I was out turning my compost pile and was startled when two field mice leaped straight up as I opened the lid. I am not a fan of mice. I shrieked, dropped the lid, and scurried away. I think they scurried away just as quickly, through a little compost 'tunnel' and out to the alley.

My church keeps a compost bin for yard scraps, and when we turned it last fall, we found several snake skins in it. I believe I would have been much more distressed by snakes crawling from my compost than by the poor little field mice that were just enjoying a snack. Fortunately, I do not have snakes in my compost because it is an enclosed bin."

CHAPTER 4

OUTDOOR
COMPOST BINS

> *"However small your garden, you must provide for two of the serious gardener's necessities: a tool shed and a compost heap."*
>
> —Anne Scott-James, gardening author, *Down to Earth*

There are a wide variety of ways to store compost as it matures, and this chapter explains several of the most common methods for creating an outdoor compost bin.

When deciding on a type of composting system, keep in mind the building materials you have available, the space you have set aside for your compost system, your building skills, and any local ordinances regarding the nature of compost containers in your neighborhood. Also, take into account the effort it will take to maintain and use each type of system. No matter what method you choose, you will most likely want a place to store materials until you can include them in the compost pile. This will help keep everything in balance and keep your compost cooking along at a healthy rate.

Do it Yourself

There are a variety of do-it-yourself methods for creating simple compost systems. The methods described here will all work if you have a yard or garden and some simple tools and materials. The cheapest and simplest methods are discussed first, followed by the more advanced kinds of bins and containers. All will yield good compost, but in differing amounts and with different investments in time, money, and energy.

Cardboard box composting

Cardboard is biodegradable and can be composted in any kind of compost system. You can also use cardboard on its own to make a temporary compost bin. This is useful if you have nowhere else to put the compost or just need a temporary storage container before moving the compost into a more permanent system. It is also good if you have accumulated more compost materials than you have room for in your regular compost bin. The box can hold the materials and allow them to break down until you have the space to move them into another bin.

Supplies

- Large cardboard box

- Four to eight bricks or rocks

Instructions

1. Open the bottom flaps of the box and set it on level ground in an out-of-the-way location with the bottom box flaps sticking out. You can set it right on top of grass; there is no need to remove the sod.

2. Weigh the box down by putting bricks or rocks on top of the extended flaps.

3. Fill the box with materials you wish to compost. Add water if the compost materials are dry, but not so much that your box disintegrates right away.

4. If you want to fold the top flaps over the compost to shield it from wind and rain, pull them out of the box before filling it with compost. Otherwise, you can tuck them inside before you fill the box. The box itself will still get wet and slowly break down.

5. When the box disintegrates so much that it can no longer contain the compost, move the compost into a regular compost container. Tear up the box and add it to the compost as well.

Wire bin composting

A wire compost bin is cheap and easy to build. It is a circular structure made of chicken wire or similar material that is placed on the ground so that worms, insects,

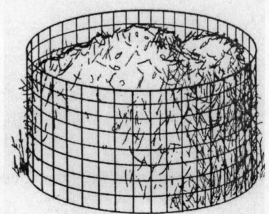

Example of a wire bin composter.
Courtesy of USDA.

and bacteria can easily enter. Its open sides provide good exposure to the air. The wire bin can be opened to access the finished compost, or you can lift the bin, move it aside, and redistribute the material back in the bin to turn it. Because this kind of compost pile is open to the elements, there is a chance it can get too wet or too dry. You should cover it during heavy rains and keep it watered during dry spells to maintain the proper level of moisture. You can also line the bin with sheets of cardboard to retain warmth and aid decomposition. A wire bin system is fairly small and will not get very hot, so it is not meant to kill off weed seeds and pathogens. Keep that in mind when filling this kind of bin.

Supplies and Tools

- Galvanized chicken wire (10 feet long and 3 feet wide)

- Heavy wire or plastic zip ties

- Four or five 3- to 4-foot-tall wooden or metal posts

- Wire snips

- Mallet

- Pliers

Instructions

1. Create an edge along each short end of the wire strip by using the pliers to fold back 3 or 4 inches of wire. This will make it safer to handle and easier to latch.

2. Shape the wire strip into a tube and place it where you want the compost pile.

3. Use the wire or plastic ties to secure the ends of the chicken wire together. Use wire if you intend to open the bin from the side. Plastic ties are all right if you plan to remove the whole wire tube from the posts to take out compost.

4. Pound the wooden posts into the ground with the mallet, making sure they are evenly spaced inside the wire tube and that they are snug against the wire.

5. To mix the compost in a wire bin, stir the mixture using an aerating tool or pitchfork. You can also pick up the bin, move it to a new location, and put the compost back into it, redistributing it as you do so.

Trash can composting

You can use ordinary household trash cans for composting, but it is harder to turn the materials in a trash can because the contents have to be dumped out and scooped back in. This is messy and

time consuming, and it also cools the compost, slowing decomposition. If the lid is secure, and the trash can is cylindrical, you can turn and roll the trash can to mix the compost. You can attach a bungee cord over the lid to keep it on if you want to try this method of mixing. A trash can looks neater than an open wire bin and might be more suitable for your location.

Example of a trash can composter.
Courtesy of USDA.

A trash can system will not get very hot, so it is not meant to kill off weed seeds and pathogens. Avoid adding any diseased plants or animal products to it.

Supplies and Tools

- Metal or plastic trash can with a lid

- Bungee cord or duct tape

- Drill with 5/16-inch drill bit

Dried leaves and twigs ready for composting.

Instructions

1. Drill rows of holes all around the trash can about 4 to 6 inches apart. These holes will allow air to flow into the compost.

2. Drill several holes in the bottom of the trash can. These holes will allow excess moisture to drain out of the can and will allow small organisms to enter the compost and help break it down.

3. Line the bottom of the can with wood chips or straw to facilitate drainage and absorb moisture. Layer in the compost materials, alternating brown and green materials.

4. Secure the lid to the can with the bungee cord or duct tape.

5. Roll the can on the ground to aerate the contents. You can do this on a schedule that suits you — every week or two, or just when the contents seems to be going anaerobic. You will know by the smell if it has started to go off.

6. You may want to remove the lid and check the moisture level periodically. If it is very dry, water it. If it is too wet, add more dry brown materials, or roll it to make sure the moisture is evenly distributed.

USE CAUTION WHEN DIGGING!

Before digging a hole or trench, check with utility companies or local authorities to make sure you will not be digging into gas lines, water mains, or electrical lines. Most states have a toll-free number you can call or a website where you can make a request for someone to come out and mark any gas, water, or electrical lines. Some require a few days notice, so make sure to call them at least a week or so before you plan to dig so that they have time to mark the lines for you. In some states, you are required by law to call ahead of time. The authority will give you a date when you are allowed to begin work, and you must work within the time frame specified.

Trench composting

Trench composting requires a patch of ground where you can dig trenches of whatever size you need to accommodate your compost. Using this method, dirt dug from the trench is used for planting while composted items are kept in a trench near the plants. As the compost items break down, they leach minerals and other nutrients into the soil beside the plants. The compost also serves to keep the area near the plants moist. A trench system will not get very hot and is not meant to kill off weed seeds and pathogens. You should also avoid placing diseased plants or animal products in this kind of compost system. This kind of composting may attract animals if you do not cover the compost promptly. Because you will be using the dirt dug up from the trench for planting, you may have to use dirt from elsewhere on the property to cover the compost as you add it to the trench. If you do not cover the compost, be aware that animals may visit and steal food items out of it. This generally is not a bad thing unless you have creatures like rats, skunks, or other undesirable animals in your area.

Supplies and Tools

- Garden spade

Instructions

1. To create a trench compost system, create a row about 3 feet wide. Divide the row into three 1-foot-wide trenches, A, B, and C. Each trench should be 8 to 10 inches deep and can be as long as you want to make it.

2. Dig a trench in row A, putting all the dirt in row C and leaving a walking space (row B) between the trench and the dirt mound.

3. Plant flowers or vegetables on the resulting dirt mound along row C.

4. Begin layering compost materials into the trench (A).

5. Use the empty space between the trench and the plants (B) for a walking path.

A (compost trench)   B (walking path)   C (planting row)

1st season

6. The following season dig up the dirt where the plants were (C) and cover the previous year's compost trench (A). Row A will be the new walking path.

7. Start composting in the new trench (C) formed in Step 6 when you dug up the plants.

8. Plant flowers or vegetables where the walking path was the previous year (B).

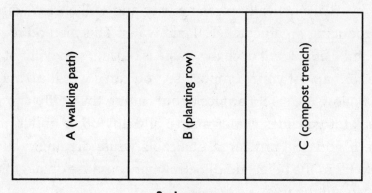

A (walking path)   B (planting row)   C (compost trench)

2nd season

9. In the third year, move the plants to the previous year's walking path and dig a trench where the plants were.

A (planting row)	B (compost trench)	C (walking path)

3rd season

10. Continue moving the trench year to year or move the compost to another area of the property where the soil needs enriching.

Trench composting in a dry environment

If you live in a very dry environment, such as a desert, or an area with very compacted subsoil, you can use trench composting to bury smelly, wet, or weedy waste. This will dispose of the waste in an aesthetically pleasing way and will enrich your soil by introducing organic material and water. This method requires some initial effort, but once the waste is buried, you will not need to turn or harvest your compost, so you can cover it up and forget it. Follow the safety advice about calling the utility company to check for gas lines, water mains, and any other underground cables. If you find any large tree roots while digging, you may want to fill in the hole, and dig elsewhere because damaging tree roots can kill the tree.

Supplies and Tools

- Digging fork

- Piece of rebar for making holes in hard soil and for prying out large rocks **Rebar** is a steel bar used to reinforce concrete and masonry structures. It comes in various sizes from ½ inch to ⅝ inch and can be found at any hardware store.

- Garden spade

- Mattock or pick for digging up or breaking rocks A **mattock** is a digging tool similar to a pick. It can have a hoe on one side of the head and a pick on the other, or an axe on one side and a pick on the other. Swing a mattock just like you would an axe.

- Heavy hammer, like a sledge hammer

- Garden hose with nearby water source, or buckets of water

Instructions

1. Use the fork to poke holes in surface turf and perforate the soil as deeply as you can. If soil is very compacted, hammer the rebar into the dirt every few inches to loosen it up.

2. Soak the area thoroughly with water and wait a day or two until the dirt softens up.

3. Dig up the topsoil and set it aside.

4. Pick out and set aside any rocks you find. If a rock is larger than your head, use the rebar to pry it out of the ground. Do not use your spade because you risk breaking the handle or the shovel portion. Use the pick or mattock to break up any rocks that seem likely to crumble.

5. Dig down at least 12 to 14 inches. A trench 24 inches deep is best because the deeper you dig, the deeper the water will penetrate and break up the compacted soil.

6. After digging as deeply as you can, pound holes into the subsoil with the rebar to allow water to infiltrate it.

7. Layer compost materials in the following order:

   a. 3 inches of coarse material such as hay, small sticks, or dead fibrous plants to help with drainage

   b. 2 inches of shredded leaves or shredded paper if you have no leaves

   c. 1 inch of soil

   d. Sprinkle the trench lightly with dry organic fertilizer and water it.

   e. 2 inches high-nitrogen material such as green grass clippings, manure, or green compost (Green compost is alfalfa or other high-nitrogen plants.)

   f. 2 inches brown ingredients (shredded paper, cardboard, small wood chips, etc.)

   g. 1 inch soil

   h. Sprinkle lightly with dry organic fertilizer and water the compost.

Continue layering in this manner until the material is 4 inches higher than ground level. Do not walk over the trench because that will compact it. You can plant in your compost pile by adding pockets of soil at least 4 inches square. You can also build a raised bed over the trench, fill it with soil and finished compost, and plant flowers in it. Watering the raised bed and the action of the plant roots will combine with the microbial action in the compost to loosen the compacted subsoil even more, allowing more water and healthy bacteria to infiltrate the soil.

If you do not plant on top of the trench, keep adding compost and mulch as the pile sinks into the trench. In the fall, dig all the plants and materials into the trench and add more soil if necessary to bring it up even with the rest of the surrounding ground. Check the pH level and amend the soil if necessary. *Instructions for checking pH with commonly available pH testing kits are in Chapter 6.* The following year, dig a new trench and repeat the process. If you do this year after year, you will eventually enrich even the driest, most inhospitable soils.

Wood trench composting

A wood trench is an above-ground, single-row version of trench composting. It is useful if you do not want to have to dig into the ground by hand, or do not want to bury the compost. The compost in a wood trench is mixed using a rototiller. A **rototiller** is a motorized cultivating machine that turns the soil with rotating blades or tines. You can rent one from an equipment rental or home improvement store. If you plan to use it often, you can purchase one. If you have a community garden, it may be something that the members want to buy and share. A wood trench system will not get very hot and is not meant to kill off weed seeds and pathogens, so do not put any diseased plants or animal products in it.

Supplies and Tools

- Post-hole digger (A **post-hole digger** is an implement used for digging holes for posts. It consists of two shovel-like blades hinged together and attached to a pair of long handles. There are also motorized post-hole diggers with

large augers. These normally require two people to operate them. You can also get post-hole digger attachments
for tractors. These are especially useful when putting up a
large fence that requires a number of holes, but might be
overkill for a small project like this.

- Four sheets of 4x8-foot exterior grade plywood

- 18 2x4 stakes, each 5 feet long

- Hammer

- Nails

Instructions

1. Bury the stakes 12 inches deep in two parallel rows, nine
    stakes to a row. Make each row 16 feet long and 2 to 3
    inches wider than your rototiller.

2. Nail the plywood sheets on the insides of the stakes, creat-
    ing a passage between them.

3. Pile compost material in a pyramid shape between the
    boards with the highest point of the pyramid in the middle
    and the sides tapering out to the open ends of the trench.
    Use the rototiller to mix the compost after it has finished
    its first cycle of heating and cooling.

When the compost has finished decaying, you can shovel it into
a pile to cure for a few weeks and re-fill the trench. **Curing** in
this context means to allow a substance (in this case compost) to
become stable. Compost is full of living organisms, so allowing it
to cure will give the microbes time to finish their job and die off
before you use the compost. You can reuse the trench over and
over until the plywood breaks down. That should not happen for

several years and when it does, you can replace the plywood and keep composting.

Hole or pit composting

Composting in a hole or pit is similar to trench composting except that the composted material is buried right away. A pit system will not get very hot and is not meant to kill off weed seeds and pathogens. There is no need to line the hole, but you should top it with a heavy lid to keep animals out while you fill it with kitchen scraps. A pit of this kind may attract flies, but a secure lid such as a heavy door or piece of plywood weighted with rocks should keep out any foraging animals.

Supplies and Tools

- Garden spade

- Lid of some kind (heavy door, sheet of plywood)

Instructions

1. Dig a hole 12 to 14 inches deep and about 20 by 36 inches long and wide.

2. Dump in the compost materials, which can include yard waste and kitchen scraps. There is no need to layer it.

3. Cover the compost with soil and pack it down. Organisms and insects in the soil will break the compost down over the course of several months to a year (depending on how much is there).

4. Cover the soil with the door or plywood to keep animals from digging up the scraps.

5. When you are ready to use the compost, you can dig it up and move it or simply plant on top of it. Make sure the compost has completely decomposed before planting any vegetables in this area because some people report that growing vegetables in unfinished compost can cause illness when they are eaten. You can plant flowers, shrubs, or any non-food items on top of the trench at any time, just be sure to add enough soil for them to root properly. Finished compost should not contain any obvious pieces of kitchen or garden scraps. It should be dark brown and crumbly and smell like fresh, clean soil.

Straw or hay bale compost piles

If you live on a farm or in a rural area, straw or old, dry hay should be easy to come by, and both are excellent materials for building your compost pile because they provide structure, insulation, and a source of carbon. Straw is most likely the cheaper option. Even in suburban areas, you should be able to find straw bales for sale at large garden centers or some farmers markets. It is often sold in the fall for Halloween and Thanksgiving decorations, so you can build your compost in

Square hay bales can be used to build a compost pile.

the fall and let it age over the winter. The following summer it should heat up nicely as long as you feed and turn it properly. This type of system, if large enough — at least 4 feet by 4 feet and at least 4 to 5 feet tall — and kept covered and properly moist, will get very warm and may kill off some weed seeds. If it is well maintained and turned regularly, it may heat up enough to kill pathogens, but do not count on this unless you are sure you will maintain it. If in doubt, do not put any diseased plants or animal products in it.

Supplies and Tools

- Nine straw or hay bales for a single bin, or 21 for a three-bin system

Instructions

1. Arrange six bales on the ground to form a U-shape with an interior space of 3 to 4 feet.

2. Along the back of the square, add another three bales to create a taller back section, overlapping the bales like bricks with one in the middle and two on either side.

3. To create a three-bin system, use six bales across the back. Create four walls of two bales each, and then place the rest of the bales across the back and on top of the walls.

Unlike wire, wooden, or concrete block compost bins, the walls of this compost bin will decay along with the contents, adding carbon to the compost pile. After several months of the composting process, the bales will be noticeably changed. At this point, you have three choices:

1. Remove the baling twine and mix the straw into the compost, making nutritious mulch for your garden. This will look like compost with straw mixed in, so it will be a dark-brown, dirt-like substance with pieces of straw.

2. Let it sit another couple of months to let the straw break down more before using it.

3. Empty the compost piles without disturbing the bales and produce another batch of compost inside them before mixing the bales into the second batch of compost.

Concrete block compost bin

Example of a cement block compost bin. Courtesy of USDA.

You can use a concrete block bin for composting or for holding compost materials that will be added to another compost bin later. This type of bin is easy to build, although it may be more expensive than a simple wire bin or a straw bale bin if you have to purchase the concrete blocks. This kind of bin is also larger and more obvious than smaller bins and is better suited for rural properties where there is more room available. Concrete block bins allow the compost to touch the ground, which is good for drainage and for introducing beneficial organisms.

The concrete blocks act as passive solar collectors and will warm up in sunlight, keeping the compost warm. Just like the straw bale compost system, a brick bin will get very warm and may kill off some weed seeds. The bin will stay warmer if it is large enough — at least 4 feet by 4 feet and at least 4 to 5 feet tall — and kept covered and properly moist. If it is very well maintained and turned regularly, it may heat up enough to kill pathogens, but do not count on this unless you are sure you will maintain it. If in doubt, do not put any animal products or diseased plants in it.

Supplies and Tools

- 46 concrete blocks for a single bin or 110 blocks for a three-bin system

- Wood or metal posts

- Mallet

Instructions

1. Line up five blocks for the back of the bin. Place blocks about ½ inch apart to allow for air flow or lay them on their sides so that the holes provide ventilation.

2. Form two rows, one at each end of the first row, to create a U-shaped bin with an open front.

3. Continue stacking the blocks, stepping them back a half step from the front and staggering them to create a three-sided block enclosure.

4. You should have enough blocks to create a bin four rows high. On the top row, you will have four blocks across the back and three on either side.

5. If you did not lay the blocks on their side in Step one, use your mallet to drive several posts through the holes in the blocks to keep the walls secure.

6. If you have 32 additional blocks, you can create another bin next to the first, with a shared wall. This second bin can be used as a holding area or a second compost area while the first bin matures. An additional 32 blocks will allow you to build a three-bin system. *Using a three-bin system is described in the next section.*

7. If you choose, you can use baby gates or a piece of fencing across the front openings to keep the compost in the bin. You may have to tie the fencing to the posts to keep it upright.

Three-bin composting

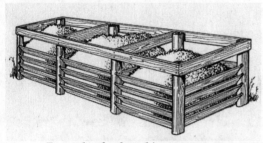

Example of a three-bin composter. Courtesy of USDA.

More advanced composters might want to construct a three-bin system. These can be made of straw bales or concrete blocks, as described previously, or they can be made from wood with various other materials. A three-bin system has many advantages because it allows you to have one bin full of materials that can be added into the compost as needed, one bin full of maturing compost, and one bin full of completed compost that is ready to be used. This means:

• You do not have to disturb the working compost pile to get to the finished compost.

- You do not have to worry about finding a place to store materials until the time is right to add them.

- You will have a continuous supply of finished compost after your first batch is done.

This type of system is more expensive to build if you have to buy wood, but often you can get free pallets or salvaged wood. This kind of system is also more useful for the dedicated gardener because of the volume of compost it can produce. A three-bin system, like the straw bin and the concrete block bin will get very warm and may kill off some weed seeds. Make sure it is large enough — at least 4 feet by 4 feet and at least 4 to 5 feet tall — and that you keep it covered and damp. A well-maintained system that is turned regularly may heat up enough to kill pathogens, but do not count on this unless you are sure you will maintain it. If in doubt, do not put any animal products or diseased plants in it.

This type of compost system consists of three bins side by side. You can make a simple and inexpensive three-bin system using ten wooden pallets (also called skids). You can often get free used pallets from stores or warehouses that are disposing of them, or you can buy them. The National Wooden Pallet and Container Association has a searchable database you can use to find a pallet vendor near you: **www.nwpca.com/SearchNew/ZipSearch.asp.**

Make sure the pallets are in good condition and wire or tie them into a series of three boxes using three pallets for the back row, four pallets to create the dividers, and three pallets for the front. This will create three adjoining boxes without a top on them. To keep the piles warm in cool climates, you can line the bins with sheets of cardboard, which will have to be replaced periodically as they break down into compost. A sheet of old carpeting can be laid over the top to keep the heat in, and the heaps can be turned every few days as they start to cool.

To build your own three-bin system from scratch, you can use various materials for the interior walls, including sheets of plywood, corrugated iron or aluminum, poultry fencing (also called chicken wire), or pieces of hardware cloth in wooden frames. These instructions will describe how to use corrugated iron or aluminum sheets, but you can use whatever works best for your situation. Pressure-treated wood is mentioned here because it is durable, but if you want to avoid the possibility of contaminating the compost with the chemicals that may leach from the wood, you can use redwood, cedar, cypress, or any other weather-hardy wood. You can also paint the wood with water-based latex paint, or coat it with linseed oil to protect it from the elements.

WHICH MATERIAL IS BEST?

A variety of materials can be used to form the walls of a wooden bin. You can use plywood, corrugated iron or aluminum, poultry fencing, pieces of hardware cloth in wooden frames, or any other sturdy material you can obtain easily. The material you use will depend on what you can get in your area, and what you feel comfortable working with. Not everyone will be at ease operating an electric saw or be able to use tin snips to cut through corrugated iron or aluminum, so use what seems best and easiest for you. The point is just to get the compost bins made and not to fret over exactly what materials they are made from.

If you are composting in order to help divert materials from a landfill, re-purposing used materials is a great way to do that. You can find used materials at second-hand shops, and at places like The Habitat Re-Store, which is a re-sale shop where you can find new and used building materials. The Re-Store (**www.habitat. org/env/restores.aspx**) is run by Habitat for Humanity. You can also often find useful materials on Freecycle.org. Freecycle is a non-profit, grassroots movement of people who are trying to keep items out of landfills. You can see if there is a Freecycle group in your area, by visiting their website: **www.freecycle.org.**

Supplies and Tools

- Post-hole digger (either manual or motor-driven)

- Garden spade

- Hammer and nails

- Drill and drill bits

- Wood screws

- Level

- String

- Tin snips

- Concrete mix (optional)

- Eight square or rectangular posts, each 5 feet long

- Four sheets of corrugated iron or aluminum, approximately 40 inches by 40 inches. They should fit between the posts.

- One sheet of corrugated iron or aluminum, approximately 10 feet long. It should fit along the back of the compost bins.

- Two 2x6s, each 8 feet long

- Two 2x2s, each 8 feet long

Instructions

1. Dig four holes in a straight line, 18 inches deep and 40 inches apart, measuring from the center of each hole.

2. Dig four more holes 40 inches in front of the holes dug in Step 1 so that you have a grid of eight holes. (Think of the pips on a die and you will have the correct placement.)

3. Insert the posts into the holes and stabilize them with concrete or by firmly packing the soil back into the holes. Use the level to ensure that the posts are level and straight. Measure the distance between the posts to make sure all the openings are the same size.

4. Using tin snips, cut a piece of corrugated iron or aluminum the same length as the entire compost bin. Attach it to the back row of posts with screws. You may have to drill through the metal first.

5. Cut four lengths of corrugated iron or aluminum to fit the ends and inner walls of the compost bin. Attach them between the posts with screws to cover the two outer walls and the two inner walls of the bin.

6. Measure between the front posts to ensure the distances are the same. Cut nine pieces from the 2x6s each ½ inch smaller than the distance between the front posts. These slats will close off the front of the bins.

7. To hold the slats in place, cut 12 pieces from the 2x2s about 14 inches long and screw them to the inner edges of the front posts, leaving a gap of at least 2 ¼ inches between them. The slats will slide between these guides to hold the compost in as it is added to the bin.

Build a tumbling barrel composter

If you have basic building skills and a few common tools, you can make your own tumbling barrel composter.

Supplies

- Two 2x4s, each 8 feet long (pressure treated to withstand the elements)

- One 1x6, 8 feet long (pressure treated to withstand the elements)

- 40 bricks (to elevate the structure off the ground)

- 16 2 ½-inch long size 8 deck screws

- One 1 ¼-inch paddle-style drill bit

- ¾-inch threaded iron pipe cut into the following lengths: one piece cut 4 feet long and two pieces 18 inches long. (You can have it cut at the hardware store because cutting threaded pipe requires specialized tools that most homeowners will not have.) * Note: Do not substitute PCV, CPVC, copper, or other types of pipe, as they are not strong enough for composters.

- Two ¾-inch threaded pipe elbows

- ¾-inch pipe cap (optional)

- 55-gallon plastic, food-grade barrel with lid (Steel drums can be used, but are more difficult to modify.)**

- Electric drill with a Phillips screw bit (or Phillips screwdriver) and ¼-inch drill bit

- Circular saw (or hand saw to cut through the 2x4s and the side of the barrel)

- File

- Vise and pipe wrench

- Four hinges 2 inches long (or one piano hinge 10 inches long) and ¼-inch bolts each 1 inch long, with nuts

- Three 1-inch lengths of 1 ½-inch plastic pipe to act as spacers (You may want to wait until the time comes to insert the spacers and measure to have a more accurate idea of how long to make them. This will vary depending on the particular barrel you have.)

- Two latches (salvaged window latches will work) and ¼-inch bolts each 1 inch long, with nuts

- One small (1 ½ inch by 1 ½ inch) repair panel or mending brace with pre-drilled holes. The photo below shows what they look like.

- 1 foot long piece of 1x1-inch angle iron and four ¼-inch bolts (each 1 inch long) with nuts

- Two ¼-inch bolts, each 2 inches long

- Measuring tape, carpenter's square or ruler, pencil, marker

To save money, buy the plain pipe, also known as black pipe. Galvanized pipe is available in this size, but at a higher cost, and the plating is not necessary for this project. You can also buy a discounted ceiling fan part for the long shaft. They are available already cut to 48 inches and threaded on one end, so they are perfect for this project.

** Food-grade barrels are steel or plastic barrels (also called drums) that have been approved to store or transport food fit for human consumption. Make sure that the barrel you use is food grade and that is has not been used to hold anything toxic. They can be purchased new or used and range widely in price. You may be able to find one free on Freecycle (**www.Freecycle.org**) or inexpensively on Craigslist (**www.Craigslist.com**) or from a scrap dealer. You can also purchase them from several online retailers for a price ranging between $10 and $250. You may also be able to purchase barrels from a hardware store, home improvement store, or farm supply store.

Instructions

The finished compost barrel.

The barrel composter is a 55-gallon drum hung horizontally on an axle. The axle has a handle at one end to turn the barrel, and the whole thing is suspended from a wooden stand. The barrel itself has a hinged opening for adding material and removing compost.

Build the legs

From each 2x4, cut two pieces each 31 inches long. (If desired, make the legs 6 inches longer so they will sit directly on the ground. In the example shown here, bricks keep the wood from touching wet soil. At this elevation, you can roll your wheelbarrow under the composter when it is time to unload the compost.)

1. Measure and mark a 1 ⅞-inch taper at one end of each piece. *Cut on the marked line as shown in Figure 1.*

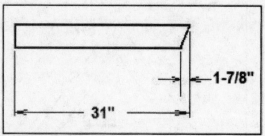

Figure 1: Diagram of 2x4 dimensions and cuts.

2. From a 1x6, cut two pieces 36 inches long. These will form the bases for the legs.

3. Lay one base board and two 2x4 legs on the floor and fit them loosely together. *Align the taper cut ends of the 2x4 legs with the base board at the bottom as in Figure 2 to make sure it all fits together.*

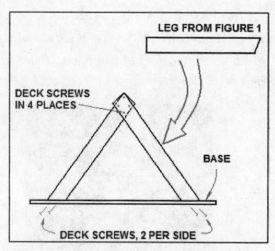

Figure 2: Diagram of one set of legs showing screws and attachment to base.

4. Align the top corners of the 2x4s and mark the screw holes as shown in Figure 2. Leave enough room between the screw holes to drill a 1 ¼-inch hole for the axle. *The location of the axle hole is shown in Figure 3.*

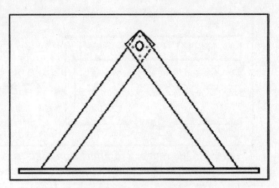

Figure 3: Diagram of one set of legs, showing placement of screw and axle holes.

5. Connect the pair of 2x4 legs together with just one 2 ½-inch long deck screw at the top. This will hold them temporarily and allow for minor corrections and adjustments later. (The screw is slightly shorter than the distance through the wood so the sharp end will not protrude.)

6. Connect the base to the legs with deck screws, using two screws per leg. Notice how the legs are stacked on top of each other and are offset at the base. *(Refer to Figure 4 to see the offset.)*

Figure 4: Side of composter showing legs, brick support, and handle.

7. Install the other three deck screws where the 2x4 legs come together at the top.

8. Using the paddle drill bit, drill a 1 ¼-inch diameter hole between the screws for the axle, situating it as shown in Figure 3. The axle, which is made of ¾-inch pipe, has an outside diameter of 1 ¹⁄₁₆ inches and so should turn smoothly in a 1 ¼-inch hole.

9. Repeat Steps 1 through 8 to make a second set of legs. Use the axle hole drilled in Step 8 to mark the location of the axle hole on the second set of legs. This will ensure that the holes are even and that the axle will not be out of alignment.

Making the axle/handle

1. *Use ¾-inch iron pipe and threaded elbow fittings to make the Z-shaped axle and handle shown in Figure 5.* Be careful when handling these pipe parts because the threaded ends can be very sharp. For best results, clamp the pipe in a vise and use a pipe wrench to turn the fittings.

2. Attach a pipe cap at the end of the handle to cover exposed threads. This will protect your hands when turning the handle. If the handle is not threaded, you will not need a pipe cap. Just be sure to smooth any sharp edges with a file.

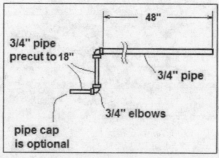

Figure 5: Diagram of axle and handle.

Prepare the barrel

1. Using a marker and carpenter's square or ruler, draw a 12x12-inch square on the side of the barrel. This will be the hatch through which you fill and empty the barrel.

2. Use your circular saw (or hand saw) to cut along the marked lines, taking care to make the cuts straight. The piece you remove will become the door of the hatch.

3. Smooth the edges with a file to avoid injury when filling or emptying the composter.

4. Add hinges to the door. Fasten either the individual hinges or the piano hinge (whichever you have) to the barrel and the door using ¼-inch nuts and bolts.

Notice how the hinge bolts work as agitators for the compost inside. *This can be seen in Figures 6 and 7 where some of the compost material has snagged on the hinges.* These pictures also show the axle running through the middle of the barrel. This helps to break up larger clumps of compost as it tumbles.

Figure 6: Photo of open composter, showing axle and compost.

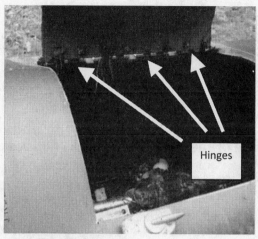

Figure 7: Photo of open composter, showing hinges and compost.

5. Install two latches to secure the door. Secure them with the same kind of ¼-inch nuts and bolts as before. *You can see detail of the latches in Figures 8 and 9.*

Figure 8: Close-up photo showing closed latch.

Figure 9: Close-up photo showing open latch and the doorstop inside the barrel.

6. Before mounting the second latch, round one corner of the door stop with the file. *You will add the stop along with one latch as shown in Figure 9, using the same bolt used to attach the latch.* The stop will keep the door from swinging into the barrel. *Figure 10 shows the metal doorstop with one corner rounded off.* (The other corners will be up against the inside of the barrel and should not pose a problem.)

Figure 10: Diagram of metal plate used as a doorstop (left) and photo of the type of plate used in this project (right).

7. Drill a 1-inch hole in each end of barrel for the axle. Center the holes on the ends of the barrel so the composter rotates evenly. To find the center of the barrel, divide the diameter by two to get the radius. Measure from the edge of the barrel toward the center and draw a line. Measure the same distance from another angle and draw another line. It is not necessary to measure at a perfect right angle when drawing these lines. The center of the circle is where the lines cross. Use this technique on both ends of the barrel. *Figure 11 shows two different ways to mark the center of the barrel. Both will work, despite the angle of the lines.*

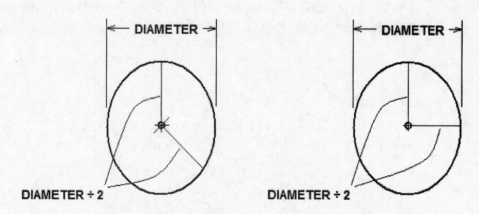

Figure 11: Diagrams showing how to mark the center of the barrel.

Connect the barrel to the axle

A piece of flat steel can be welded to the axle and bolted through the bottom end of the barrel as shown in Figure 12. However, most homeowners do not have access to welding equipment, so an alternative method is described here which uses angle iron.

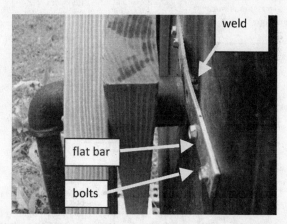

Figure 12: Photo showing attachment of barrel to frame using a flat bar welded to the axle and bolts through the bar into the barrel.

1. *Drill holes in the angle iron as shown in Figure 13.* You can do this with a household drill and ¼-inch drill bit. Drill holes 1 inch and 3 inches from each end of the iron on one side.

On the other side, drill a hole directly in the center, at the 6-inch mark.

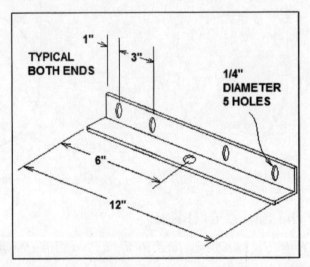

Figure 13: Diagram showing placement of drill holes in angle iron.

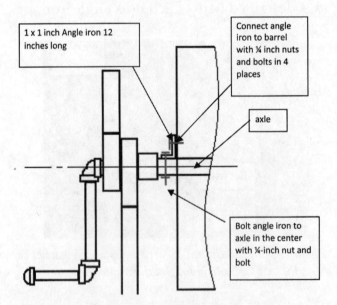

Figure 14: Diagram of handle, legs, and barrel,
showing angle iron bolted to axle and screwed to barrel.

2. Dry fit the angle iron to the axle and barrel. Make sure that the angle iron is attached to the bottom of the barrel and not the lid. Although the lid may be tightly fitted, there is a chance that it will unscrew and work its way loose as the barrel is turned.

3. Align the center hole in the angle iron with the center of the axle. Mark the holes on the barrel and the axle with a marker.

4. Drill matching ¼-inch holes through the axle and barrel on the marks.

5. Use ¼-inch bolts and nuts to connect the angle iron to the axle and barrel as shown in Figure 14.

Figure 15: Photo showing placement of spacers and retainer bolt in end of axle.

Assembling the composter

1. Cut three pieces of plastic tubing, each 1 inch long, for spacers. These spacers prevent contact between the barrel and the legs, making the composter easier to turn.

2. *Assemble the components as shown in Figure 16.*

3. Add a spacer between the leg and the side of the barrel on the end where the handle is. *This is shown in Figure 16.*

4. Add the other two spacers at the other end of the barrel, one between the barrel and the legs, and the other between the legs and the retainer bolt. *This is shown in Figures 16 and 17.* Depending on the lid of your barrel, it may be necessary to insert an additional spacer between the lid and legs on that side or to make a longer spacer to fit the gap. This is due to the different shape lids that some barrels have. Some are convex and some are concave. The concave lids bow into the barrel and will require longer or additional spacers.

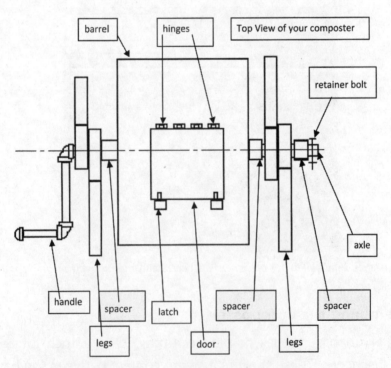

Figure 16: Diagram of the assembled composter as shown from the top.

Figure 17: Photo of side of the composter, showing the spacer between the leg and the barrel.

Start composting

1. Move your new composter to a level area. If necessary, stack bricks two levels high to elevate the composter and keep the wood from coming in contact with the ground. This will help prevent the wood from rotting. Make sure your wheelbarrow will fit under the composter so you can easily empty out the finished compost.

2. If there are children nearby, show them what you are doing and why. Explain that this composter is not a toy and is not something they should play on or around.

3. Follow the instructions in this book to create your own compost.

Commercial Outdoor Compost Bins

If you do not have the time or expertise to build your own compost system, you can purchase one from nearly any garden supply company or from a variety of online sources. They are available in a wide assortment of styles and sizes to suit any space. Commercial compost bins come in two forms: tumbling or stationary. Some cities and towns provide free or low-cost compost systems to their residents. Check with your municipal trash department if you have one, or with your town or city hall first for the most economical option and also to make sure you are aware of any municipal regulations regarding the placement and use of composters.

Tumbling bins

Most tumbling compost bins are barrel-shaped and turn either end-over-end or horizontally depending on the type. Some are operated by hand and some by foot pedal. The larger the bin, the harder it is to turn, especially when the barrel is full of composting material, so take this into account when deciding on a size and style, and choose one that you can easily manage on your own. Some tumblers are round like a ball and are mixed by pushing the ball along the ground. Because tumblers are aerated and sealed and usually elevated off the ground, you can put cooked food and a small amount of cooked meat waste into them. One drawback of this type of bin is that it does not hold enough material to get hot enough to kill weeds or pathogens.

To give you an idea of the cost, Gardener's Supply Company (**www.gardeners.com**) sells a tumbling bin that holds about 6.5 cubic feet of compost for $149 and a larger one that holds 22.4 cubic feet for $495. Some models are on wheeled stands so they can be tipped and rolled to where you need them. Others are stationary, and you must empty the compost where the tumbler sits and transport it where you need it.

Stationary bins

Stationary compost bins that sit in one place have lids on top and a compartment at the bottom to remove the finished compost. Some types of stationary bins are self-aerating.

There are a few types of stationary bins.

- The Dalek type, which is smaller on top than on the bottom and resembles the alien race from the television show *Doctor Who*. This is the sort of bin that is often available inexpensively from city or town composting groups. Dalek-type composters come in a range of sizes, but there are limits on what should be put into them. Unlike hot compost heaps, these plastic bins cannot handle any form of cooked food, meat, or other animal products. They should not be used to compost diseased plants because they do not get hot enough to kill the pathogens.

- The Green Johanna™ Hot Komposter is shaped similarly to the Dalek type, but allows you to compost a wider variety of items including meat, fish, and bones. This style of composter was designed for the cold climate in Sweden and can heat compost up to 150 degrees. You can stir this kind of bin with an aerating tool and can purchase an optional cover (called a jacket or a duvet, depending on where you live). Green Johanna™ composters have reinforced, rat-proof bottoms, making them a good choice for areas where pests might be a problem.

- The New Zealand type, which resembles a large upright barrel and contains three inner chambers, composts scraps in stages. Stage one is the warmest stage where thermophilic microorganisms break the material down. In stage two, the mesophilic microorganisms kick in and compost the materials further. In the final stage, the compost matures and can be scooped out for use. This type goes by the brand name Earthmaker®.

- Self-aerating compost bins resemble barrels or trash containers. They often have a pipe jutting up from the bottom of the bin that allows air into the center of the pile. The base of this kind of bin is perforated to allow liquid to seep out of the bin and to allow air to come in. On some models, this liquid can be collected and made into compost tea. *Chapter 6 discusses making and using compost tea.*

- Some stationary bins are pyramid-shaped and consist of stacking layers and a perforated lid that allows rainwater to enter and dampen the compost. One brand of pyramid-shaped bin is called the Eco Stack™ Composter. After the bin is filled, you remove the sections of the bin one at a time, setting them aside, then fork the compost back in to finish decomposing. This particular brand does not require turning because it self-aerates through holes in the bottom of the bin. It can take more than a year to produce usable compost using this type of bin.

All of these bins are good for small yards and some can be used on balconies. They are also good for people who may not have the strength or ability to turn a tumbling model. The self-aerating models, although usually more expensive (in the $400 range) are probably the easiest to use because you do not have to mix the compost by hand or by tumbling.

Digesters

A **digester** consists of a basket with holes in it that is buried in the ground and has a tall plastic cone that fits over it. You add waste through the top of the cone, and insects and microorganisms in the soil decompose the waste into compost under the surface of the ground. Liquid waste drains into the soil and worms, and insects carry away some of the solid waste. The digester has to be moved every couple of years, depending on how often you use it, to prevent the compost from building up in one place. The compost usually is not dug up from where it is created, so this is a good way to enrich small areas of soil. Digesters can take any kind of kitchen scraps, including cooked meat and fish, cheese, and other cooked foods.

You can make your own digester by drilling holes in the sides and bottom of a metal trash can and burying it in the ground. Let a few inches of the trash can stick up out of the ground; fasten the lid with a bungee cord or other method to keep animals out. Make sure the spot you choose drains well and does not have too much clay. High clay content will prevent the liquid waste from seeping into the surrounding soil. When the trash can is full, you will have to dig it up, empty the remaining compost into the ground, and cover the hole with dirt. Move the can to another area of the yard that needs enriching and start composting again.

Whether you make a bin or buy one, composting is a fun and important pastime. It gives you the satisfaction of recycling waste, helps divert organic materials from landfills, and helps your garden grow. Before diving into composting, think about the different types of composting systems discussed, and choose one that will work for you. *If you do not have a yard or garden, be sure to check out Chapter 7 on vermicomposting and the sections of Chapter 8 on indoor composting to see if one of those methods will work better for you.*

If you plan to do outdoor composting, however, read on to find out how to build effective compost piles.

CASE STUDY

Linda Stephenson
Amateur composter
Santa Cruz, California

"My 'garden' is the small front yard of my rented house, and not a place where I can freely experiment with plantings. Santa Cruz has just been through a severe drought, with equally severe water rationing. Fortunately, the xerophytic landscape came through well, and looks none the worse now after a wet winter. (**Xerophytic landscaping** is the use of plants that can survive with very little water. It is practiced in desert areas and towns and cities that rely on water from distant sources.)

Enriching the soil with compost has not been a goal here, but I have composted with worms and without worms for many years in order to keep garbage out of the landfill. I do not have room for a big compost pile, so I just use the worm bin. I give the worms most of our family's vegetable waste including peelings, cores, abandoned leftovers, and used coffee grounds and filters. The compost I have made in past years was just spread in the back yard, where a few citrus trees struggled for light. Now that I have no back yard, I usually spread the worm castings under a grapefruit tree on the side of the house.

I have to keep the front yard looking neat and tidy, so I bought a tidy-looking vermiculture contraption from the local recycling company that subsidizes all its composters. It is plastic, but looks like stone, and is not conspicuous. It is a stack of three, 14-inch-square bins, each 6 inches deep, over a sealed bottom box, and it has a slanted cover that fits tightly over all. Each individual bin has drainage holes. I moved a cardboard box full of red wrigglers from our old house to the new house and put them in the new worm bin. I keep the stacked worm bin at ground level on the side of the deck where it is mostly in the shade. Our climate is mild year-round, so the worms are happy in there.

The general idea was to start the worms in the bottom bin in some torn and dampened newspaper and keep adding vegetable waste until that bin was full of finished worm castings. Then, to make it easier for me (rather than having to manually separate the worms from their castings), I could start putting food waste in the next bin up, and hope the worms would migrate up to the food. That was the idea, but it has never worked terribly well. They seem reluctant to move, even when their food source gets sparse. I end up doing a good bit of manual sorting, because I cannot bear to dump out perfectly healthy little worms into an environment they can't survive in. Red wrigglers do not do well in ordinary garden soil.

I compost because it is pleasant to do. I do not have a smelly garbage can to deal with, I do not needlessly fill up the landfill, and I am fond of the hungry little fellows. If I buy a bunch of cilantro and fail to use it before it spoils, I take some comfort out of feeding it to the worms instead of wasting food. When my kids were young, they liked to help me feed the worms to keep them healthy and watch how they multiplied when conditions were good. The red wrigglers were just another creature that we enjoyed having around — along with silk worms and a succession of small rodents, cats, and a dog.

Sometimes I miscalculate and overfeed the worms. When I have miscalculated, the worm bin has gotten gooey, smelly, and unpleasant to deal with. When that happens, I have to discard the household waste in the garbage can until the worms have a chance to catch up.

CHAPTER 5

BUILDING A COMPOST PILE

You will need some basic tools and supplies to build and maintain your compost pile. You may already have some or most of these in your home or garage. If not, you can find them at most hardware stores, home improvement centers, and gardening supply stores, or you can buy them online. You may also be able to get them free, or at least inexpensively, at thrift stores, garage sales, flea markets, Craigslist, or Freecycle.

Tools for Digging and Raking

Outdoor composting involves a lot of digging, chopping, and raking, so you will want sturdy, well-balanced tools. Here is some information on various tools you will need and some that are just nice to have.

Shovels or garden spades

These come with straight blades, pointed blades, and rounded blades. Select the type that works best for you. You may want to have one of each. A straight, or squared-off, blade lets you easily chop through coarse, matted compost. A pointed blade will make it easier to dig into heavy clay soil. Looser soils can be dug easily with a round-bladed shovel.

Make sure the blade is made of forged steel and is not a flimsier stamped metal. Forged steel is created by dropping a heavy mechanized hammer onto a piece of steel to shape it, usually in a mold. Stamped metal shovel heads are created by cutting a shovel-shaped stamp out of a sheet of metal and bending it into shape. Forging creates a much stronger tool, which will make digging easier. In addition, the tool will last longer. It is also important to keep the blade sharp. A dull blade will not do its job and will force you to work harder to accomplish the same task. You can sharpen shovel blades with a simple metal file. You should sit comfortably and hold the shovel blade in a position that will let you run the file across the concave edge of the shovel. (This is the side where you would hold dirt if you were digging with it.) About 20 strokes should be enough to sharpen the blades. You can also sharpen the back, but this is not usually necessary. You should do this after several hours of digging. If you cannot remember the last time you sharpened the blade, it is probably time to do it again.

Hoes

A straight-edged hoe is the most useful for composting because its sharp blade helps you break up composted materials. Some special types of hoes are designed for weeding gardens. Warren hoes come with pointed blades. The stirrup hoe blade resembles a stirrup on a saddle. If you have a vegetable garden, you may want to use one of these specialty hoes, but for composting purposes, an ordinary garden hoe is best.

Rakes

There are two general kinds of rakes — leaf rakes and garden rakes. **Leaf rakes** are designed to rake a lot of leaves quickly. You can also use them to rake grass clippings and other lightweight items. They have wide, claw-like heads made of thin metal tines. The tines resemble fingers with the tips bent at a 90-degree angle. Some tines have rubber tips that protect hard surfaces like pavement and decks. Some leaf rakes have adjustable heads so that you can make them narrower to fit into small spaces. Leaf rakes are generally lightweight and can be made of plastic, metal, bamboo, and other materials. When buying a rake, make sure that the tines are sturdy enough to withstand regular use and that the head is firmly attached to the handle. **Garden rakes** are used for spreading gravel or dirt and other heavy-duty jobs. They usually have a wooden handle and a metal head about 12 to 18 inches wide. The end of the head has 2- to 3-inch long teeth. Modern rakes may have fiberglass handles. This makes them lighter weight and easier to handle. You will only need a garden rake if you have a garden or are installing a garden path or other feature that requires moving a lot of dirt or stone.

Forks

If you have an outdoor compost heap you will spend a lot of time turning the compost pile, and a fork is the best tool for this job. **Pitchforks** have long, sharp tines that can easily pierce through materials and lift clumps of compost ingredients. These tines are spaced a few inches apart, so they may not be the best bet for lifting more mature compost, which is composed of smaller pieces. **Manure forks** are similar to pitchforks, but have more tines that are spaced closer together. They are designed for digging and moving manure piles and are ideal for doing the same with compost. Smaller **digging forks** feature thicker tines and are very useful for turning compost, digging holes, and piercing compost piles to allow air infiltration. These sturdy forks are probably the best type to buy if you can afford only one fork.

Mattocks

If you need to dig into very firmly compacted dirt or chop through branches or roots, a mattock is the tool you want. Mattocks come in various configurations, but all have a heavy metal head on a short wooden handle, similar to an axe handle. The head of the mattock will have a hoe on one side and a pick or an axe on the other side of the head. These tools should be swung like axes and are useful for chopping apart compost or prying rocks out of holes in the ground.

Post-hole diggers

When building a compost bin, you may need to dig holes to bury corner posts, such as when making a wooden single- or triple-bin system. You might also want to erect a fence around a certain area of your yard to block the view of the compost pile. A post-hole digger is an implement used for digging holes for posts. It consists of two shovel-like blades hinged together and attached to a pair of long handles. There are also motorized post-hole diggers with large augers. These normally require two people to operate them. Post-hole diggers also are available as tractor attachments. The motorized and tractor-mounted types can usually be rented from home improvement stores or equipment rental stores.

A VIBRANT GUIDE TO
COMPOSTING

WHERE DO I COMPOST?

Stationary Compost Container

There are many different types of compost systems available for gardeners interested in composting. There are different drawbacks and benefits to each, so every gardener must determine for themselves what will work best in the space they have. For instance, you may prefer to have your compost in an exposed heap to make it easier to mix, or you may like to keep it in a bin to preserve the aesthetics of your yard.

Wooden Compost Bin

Compost Heap

Concrete Compost Bin

Compost Hole

Aside from the traditional compost pile and compost bin, there is also the tumbling barrel composting system. They are designed to allow air into the compost, and the tumbling action helps to mix the ingredients. However, you must be careful when choosing your barrel, as some models can be difficult to turn and empty.

Tumbling Barrel

WHAT CAN I COMPOST FROM MY YARD?

Wool

Dead Plants

If you have a garden or even just a yard, you already have materials that you can add to your compost bin. Dead plants and clippings from your lawn or bushes compost well. If you keep farm animals, you can also use their feathers, wool, or even their manure, depending on the type of animal.

Wood Ash

Poultry Feathers

WHAT CAN I COMPOST FROM MY KITCHEN?

Tea Leaves

Coffee Grounds

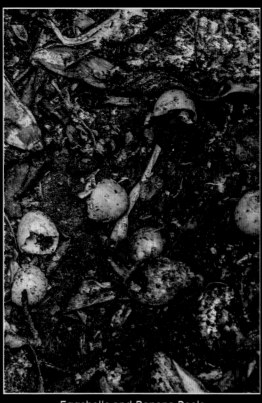
Eggshells and Banana Peels

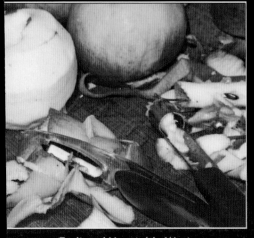
Fruit and Vegetable Waste

A large amount of food waste can be composted. Instead of throwing away your used coffee grounds and vegetable peels, keep them in a separate, sealed container that you can then empty every so often into your compost pile. You can also add moldy bread and rotted food into your compost, and give new life to your expired goods instead of just throwing them in the trash.

WHAT CAN I COMPOST FROM MY HOME?

Newspaper

Wrapping Paper

Many items that you would otherwise recycle or toss into the trash can be used in composting. Several types of paper, including shredded office paper, wrapping paper and newspaper can be composted. If composting seashells or crustacean shells, be sure to crush the shells well so that they break down quicker.

Crushed Seashells

Yarn

WHAT PLANTS SHOULD I KEEP OUT OF MY COMPOST BIN?

Morning Glory

You should never introduce anything into your compost that you do not want to spread into your garden. For this reason, you should avoid putting diseased plants into your compost pile. Though the plant may break down fine, the disease pathogen may still be able to spread to other plants. You'll also want to avoid invasive weeds as, if allowed to spread, they may destroy your garden.

Diseased Plants

Sheep Sorrel

WHAT ITEMS SHOULD I KEEP OUT OF MY COMPOST BIN?

Rubber

Coal Ash

Although you can toss most of your household waste into your compost bin, there are some items you should definitely avoid. Unlike wood ash, coal ash is bad for your soil and will poison it if introduced to the compost heap. Other items may take a very long time to break down or attract vermin as they decompose, so it is best to check before just throwing your waste in with your compost.

Cooked Food and Meats

Dairy Products

Compost
"Compost after sieving, ready for application (8916542948)"
by SuSanA Secretariat - https://www.flickr.com/photos/gtzeco-
san/8916542948/. Licensed under CC BY 2.0 via Wikimedia Commons
- http://commons.wikimedia.org/wiki/File:Compost_after_sieving,_
ready_for_application_(8916542948).jpg#/media/File:Compost_af-
ter_sieving,_ready_for_application_(8916542948).jpg

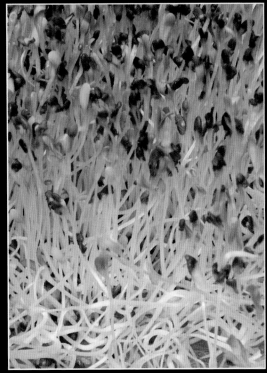

Alfalfa
"Graines de luzerne bio germées - 002" by Thesupermat - Own
work. Licensed under CC BY-SA 3.0 via Wikimedia Commons -
http://commons.wikimedia.org/wiki/File:Graines_de_luzerne_bio_
germ%C3%A9es_-_002.JPG#/media/File:Graines_de_luzerne_bio_
germ%C3%A9es_-_002.JPG

Bone Meal

Activators are substances that can help the composting process begin. There are many natural types of activators, including alfalfa meal, manure, bone meal, and old compost. You could also use a chemical fertilizer as long as you ensure that there is enough carbon-rich material to counteract it.

HOW DO I KNOW MY COMPOST PILE IS THRIVING?

Bats

Toads

Beetles

There are many organisms responsible for decomposing the materials in a compost heap. Fungi, molds and bacteria do the bulk of this work but larger organisms such as snails, beetles and worms also contribute. If your compost pile is healthy, the presence of these organisms should attract larger creatures as well, such as toads, birds and bats.

Snails

TOOLS FOR A SUCCESSFUL COMPOST SYSTEM

Before you start composting, it is important that you obtain the basic tools necessary to build and maintain your compost system. There is a great deal of digging and raking involved in composting, so be sure to purchase sturdy tools that can handle use well.

Mattock

Rake

Garden Hoe

KEEPING UP WITH THE COMPOST HEAP

Thermometer

Once you've gotten your composting system built, you'll need to maintain it. Compost thermometers are necessary so that you may turn your compost once you see that it has started to cool. You'll also need to ensure that your compost pile is staying moist and be able to measure that level of moisture so you can prevent it from getting too wet.

Aeration Pump

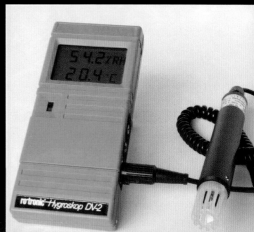

Humidity Meter

WORMING INTO THE GARDEN

Vermicomposting is a very effective method of composting. By introducing worms into your compost system, you allow for more worm castings to enhance you compost. They are high in calcium, iron, phosphorous and nitrogen and are effective at killing fungal spores that can otherwise infect your more delicate plants.

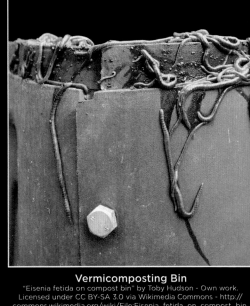

Vermicomposting Bin
"Eisenia fetida on compost bin" by Toby Hudson - Own work. Licensed under CC BY-SA 3.0 via Wikimedia Commons - http://commons.wikimedia.org/wiki/File:Eisenia_fetida_on_compost_bin.jpg#/media/File:Eisenia_fetida_on_compost_bin.jpg

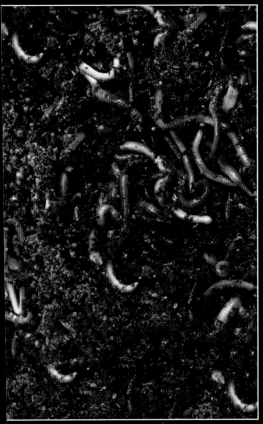

Red Wigglers

Dew Worm

WHAT TO FEED YOUR WORMS

Bread

Worms can eat most foods that you would put into a compost heap. They enjoy stale bread as well as leftover pasta. When feeding worms, it is important to incorporate a source of grit into their diet. You can do this by adding ground eggshell to your worm bin or even sand.

Corn Meal

Vegetables

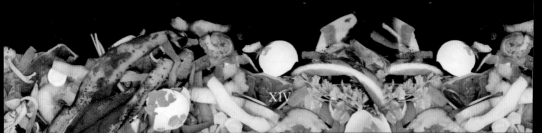

WHAT NOT TO FEED YOUR WORMS

Citrus Peels
"WikiGrenier 20150227 - citron vert du Mexique 8" by Lionel Allorge - Own work. Licensed under CC BY-SA 3.0 via Wikimedia Commons - http://commons.wikimedia.org/wiki/File:WikiGrenier_20150227_-_citron_vert_du_Mexique_8.jpg#/media/File:WikiGrenier_20150227_-_citron_vert_du_Mexique_8.jpg

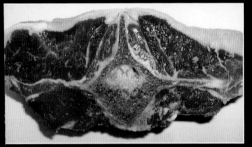

Raw Meat

Hot Peppers

If you plan on using worms in your composting system, then it is important that you take care with what waste items you put into your bins. Worms avoid eating seeds, so it is best not to give them fruits or vegetables with seeds, as plants may start growing in your bin. In addition, citrus peels can be poisonous to worms and a surplus of citrus may even change the pH of the soil, making the bin inhospitable for worms.

Cucumbers
"HK SYP Best of Best Vegetable green Cucumbers Aug-2012" by Genmewcaugsa - Own work. Licensed under CC BY-SA 3.0 via Wikimedia Commons - http://commons.wikimedia.org/wiki/File:HK_SYP_Best_of_Best_Vegetable_green_Cucumbers_Aug-2012.JPG#/media/File:HK_SYP_Best_of_Best_Vegetable_green_Cucumbers_Aug-2012.JPG

Flower Beds

Flower Pots

Vegetable Gardens

Compost can be used everywhere in your garden. Spread a layer of compost near any plants that look like they need a boost of nutrients. Compost helps prevent your plants from getting diseases and allows them to retain more water.

Tools for Storing and Moving Compost

When you gather compost ingredients, you will need some place to store them temporarily until you can dump them into the pile or bin. You can collect kitchen waste in any sort of waterproof container that has a tight fitting lid (to reduce odor and keep flies out). Moving larger amounts of ingredients, such as yard waste requires wheelbarrows, garden carts, or even large tarps used as a sling. **Wheelbarrows** require you to balance the load on a single wheel and lift the load at the same time, which can be tricky. **Garden carts** support more of the weight of the load on the two wheels, and no balancing act is involved. A **tarp** is useful for dragging a large, light pile of ingredients, such as leaves or weeds, and the tarp itself takes up almost no storage space once it has been folded.

WHAT IS THE DIFFERENCE BETWEEN A WHEELBARROW AND A GARDEN CART?

A wheelbarrow has only one, centrally placed wheel while a garden cart has two wheels and usually has a larger, flatter storage area. Which you choose depends on the job you are performing. A pile of compost or dirt can be transported in either one, but a wheelbarrow generally has a rounded front that makes it easier to pour things out of it. Garden carts are usually more box-like and better for transporting things like flowerpots, buckets, and other garden gear, although some of them do have sloped bodies similar to wheelbarrows. Some garden carts can be folded up for storage, as can some wheelbarrows, whose bodies are made of a sling-like tarp attached to a wheel.

Tools for Cutting

A lot of cutting happens in a garden. You have to cut string on bales of straw, cut vegetables and fruits off the vine, cut dead branches off trees, cut down weeds and grass, cut up old cardboard boxes to use in compost bins, or cut fence wire to make or repair wire composters or compost sifters. Compost ingredients also have to be chopped, crushed, or otherwise reduced to smaller pieces so there is a larger surface area for bacteria to work on. A few common tools will make these jobs easier.

Knife

A sturdy, sharp knife is useful all over the garden. From cutting string to slicing a warm tomato on a hot summer day, knives are indispensable garden tools. You can get knives with all sorts of fancy attachments, so take your time choosing one. Make sure if fits your hand and that you are comfortable using it. Invest in a sheath or a large magnet mounted on the wall of your garden shed or side of your garden cart so you can find it.

Scissors

Kitchen scissors will cut up nearly any kind of kitchen waste or soft garden scraps. They will also cut through plastic or fabric, such as bags containing soil amendments or compost additives.

Hammer

Some fibrous compost ingredients break down more easily if you hammer them flat first. Use a hammer to pound corncobs, small tree branches, and other tough ingredients before putting them into the compost. A hammer is also useful for pounding loose nails back into compost bins. A framing hammer with a steel handle will last forever.

Machete

A machete will make short work of yard waste. Use it for chopping vines, old vegetables, small hedge trimmings, and anything else that needs to be chopped. To be safe, keep it sharp and use it on a flat wooden surface such as a tree stump or butcher's block. You can sharpen a machete yourself with a mill file. (This is a common steel file that you can buy at any hardware store.) To sharpen your machete, clamp it by the handle in a vise with the blade pointing straight up and with the sharp edge away from you. You may also hold the handle of the machete in your hand. Stroke the file away from you and along the blade at a very shallow angle. Your fingers should almost touch the side of the blade. If your machete does not have a hand guard, you may want to leave a few inches unsharpened near the handle in case your hand slips during use. Repeat this on the other side. If you do not feel comfortable sharpening a machete yourself, take it to a knife-sharpening shop.

Compost Maintenance Tools

You can make perfectly good compost with the tools listed so far, but you may want to have a few more specialized tools on hand. These help with maintaining the proper balance of air, water, and heat in your compost.

Thermometer

You normally turn compost as soon as it starts to cool down and a thermometer will let you see how hot your pile is getting (so you will know if your "hot heap" is truly hot) and will tell you when the temperature is dropping. Compost thermometers come in a wide range of sizes, styles, and prices, but in general, they all have a long metal probe attached to a gauge.

Example of a composting thermometer. Temperatures can reach 150 degrees or more; be careful and use gloves at all times.

Watering tools

A moisture meter will tell you if your compost is damp enough in the middle. In addition to monitoring the moisture level, you can make watering easier by burying soaker hoses right in the compost pile. You can buy a soaker hose, use an old leaky hose, or use a hose into which you have poked holes. Make sure to use a moisture meter if you go this route, so that the pile does not get too wet. These are similar to compost thermometers and feature a gauge on the end of a long metal probe with a moisture sensor on the end. These devices can be purchased from garden supply stores or online and range in price from about $10 to about $250. They also come in several different lengths, so you can measure all the way to the center of your compost pile.

Aerators

An outdoor compost pile or heap can be turned with a digging fork or shovel, but smaller compost bins require the use of aerators. These tools turn, mix, and stir the compost to let air in, which keeps your aerobic bacteria alive. Aerators are normally long metal stakes with either a screw-shaped end (like an auger) or a spring-loaded end that enters the compost smoothly and then pops open little wing-like extensions when you pull back on it.

Safety Equipment

While composting is not an inherently dangerous activity, you should still take some precautions. This equipment will help prevent injury and, in some cases, diseases that you can contract from handling certain materials.

Gloves

Gloves are the most basic piece of safety equipment. Always wear gloves when working with compost that contains any kind of manure or food waste. You may want the rubber-coated gardening gloves for this and other wet, messy tasks. You can wear ordinary cotton gardening gloves to protect your hands from blisters when shoveling, raking, and doing other repetitive jobs. Sturdy leather gloves will also help you avoid splinters and accidental pricks from thorns while gathering yard waste. Keep gloves clean and dry. If you have any open wounds on your hands (even something as small as a paper cut or bloody hangnail), cover it with a bandage and consider wearing rubber gloves under your cotton gloves.

Dust masks

Dust masks are important when you are working with any dry powdery material that you might inhale. Old straw and hay can contain disease-causing fungal spores. It is also possible to inhale powdered compost activators and ingredients, such as powdered limestone and rock dust. If you suffer from plant allergies, wearing a mask while working with yard waste (shredding leaves or chopping stalks) can help minimize your exposure to pollen. Also, make sure to wear a dust mask while sawing any wood.

Goggles

Goggles will protect your eyes while doing tasks such as chipping or sawing wood or chopping or pounding yard waste. You should also wear goggles when pounding nutshells and seashells with your hammer. This precaution will help avoid unpleasant trips to the emergency room.

Ear protection

Ear protection is important when running loud equipment, such as wood chippers, lawn mowers, string trimmers, or leaf shredders. You can wear expandable foam earplugs or ear protectors, which resemble large headphones.

Compost Ingredients

All compost piles require the same balance of nutrients — approximately 25 to 30 parts carbon to one part nitrogen, or 25 to 30 parts brown to one part green. This can vary depending on how fast or slow you want the compost pile to decompose. If you want a slower pile, add more brown, carbon-rich items. If you want a faster pile, increase the amount of green or nitrogen-rich items. But in general, a ratio of 25 to 30 parts brown to one part green is a good, workable ratio for all types of compost systems.

After you have built or purchased your compost system, you will need to gather and store the green and brown raw materials. It is easy to store brown materials because they are generally dry and do not rot. You can put these in an empty bay of a three-bin compost system, or in a separate container. You can also pile them up

in boxes, trash cans, or whatever container is handy. Green materials are harder to store because they tend to rot if piled up. It is best to collect green materials as close to the time of building the pile as possible.

Depending on the type of composting you are doing, you may be able to dump ingredients into your compost as you accumulate them. For example, most stationary outdoor bins, digesters, worm bins, and electric indoor bins let you add materials at any time. An open compost heap that rarely gets turned can also handle a bit more variation in content. However, if you are trying to generate compost systematically, it is best to keep the proper ratio in mind and only add ingredients when you have the correct proportion of one part green to 25 or 30 parts brown.

How do I know if I have the right ratio?

If you are worried that your ratio of browns to greens will not be exactly "correct," you can weigh all your materials, but that is not really practical. A simpler way is to measure the materials using whatever you have on hand. For example, get five 5-gallon buckets. Fill them over the course of a few weeks with brown materials, such as shredded paper, cardboard tubes from toilet tissue or paper towels, dry chopped grasses or plant stocks, dry brown leaves, and whatever other carbon sources you have on hand. When you have collected five 5-gallon buckets full of brown materials, begin collecting green materials from your kitchen and garden in a 1-gallon container such as a large coffee can, or a regular household bucket. A covered container is recommended for this just to keep the flies out. After you have filled the 1-gallon container with green materials, you will automatically have a 25-gallon to 1-gallon ratio of browns to greens, and you will be able to fill your compost container with the correct balance all at once.

Slow or Cool Compost

Remember, composting will proceed as quickly as you want it to, depending on the materials you use and how you manage the compost pile. If you are not in a hurry, do not have time to tend to the compost pile, or have a very large quantity of carbon-rich items (such as a large pile of wood chips), you can make slow compost. As with any other kind of compost, you simply layer the brown and green ingredients and give them a stir every once in awhile.

For slow compost use a much larger concentration of carbon-rich material. A normal ratio is about one part green to 25 or 30 parts brown, so for a slower compost pile you should increase the amount of carbon material significantly, even up to 200 parts carbon (brown) material to one part nitrogen (green) material. By decreasing or eliminating the greens altogether, you can create a compost pile that can take years to decompose. You can stir it, but you do not have to. If there is little to no green material providing nitrogen, the microbial activity should slow down dramatically, and there should be no problem with odor or excessive wetness. A slow compost system will not get very hot and will not kill weeds or pathogens. It should not be used for composting meat, animal waste, or diseased plants. You can start a slow compost pile in the fall when you do your final yard cleanup. Use fallen leaves, old plant stalks, spoiled garden vegetables, shredded branches, and other high-carbon materials. Pile these up along with household waste, and let it begin to compost over the winter. By spring, you will have a pile of partially decayed compost that can be the beginnings of a fresh compost heap.

Medium or Warm Compost

Materials will compost even if you get the balance slightly wrong or do not stir or turn the materials. Most gardeners want to create compost in a reasonable amount of time, and a normal household compost system can produce good compost in three to nine months, depending on how it is cared for and the climate where it is built.

These instructions will give you the basics of building a standard or medium speed compost pile sufficient for most households. This system will get very warm, but it may not get hot enough to kill weeds and pathogens and should not be used for composting any animal waste or diseased plants.

The compost materials do not have to be added all at once. Start the pile when you have enough browns and greens for two layers. You can always add more layers as you accumulate materials.

Supplies and tools

Depending on the size of your compost system, you may need tools to transport and move all your items into place. You also will need a bin made of wire, wood, concrete blocks, or straw bales.

- A wheelbarrow

- Spades and shovels

- Garden fork or aerator

- Buckets

- Brown and green compost ingredients

- Manure or activator

Instructions

1. Start with a brown, fibrous layer on the bottom, about 6 inches deep. This will allow air to circulate under the pile and will give liquids a place to drain so that they do not overwhelm the bacteria and lead to anaerobic decomposition.

2. Add a layer of green materials about 2 inches deep.

3. *Add a thin layer of activator such as manure or one of the types of meal discussed in Chapter 2.*

4. Repeat the layers until the pile is at least 4 to 5 feet tall. If you do not have enough material to do this all at once, add layers as you accumulate ingredients.

5. When the pile heats up (usually after three to four days if you build the pile all at once), use a pitchfork to move the outer layers to the inside and the inside layers to the outside. Mix it up well and let it sit for a few more days or weeks as your schedule dictates. Turning the pile less frequently will mean slower decomposition, while turning it too often (while the pile is very hot and active) will cool the pile and will delay decomposition.

Fast or Hot Compost

Hot compost.

If you want to make compost quickly, you can use the University of California method. This hot heap method will generate usable compost in two weeks. The compost produced will be rough, in both texture and the degree to which it is complete, but you can use it right away for mulching and it should finish decomposing on the ground by the end of the season. To use this method, you will need some kind of outdoor compost structure, such as a straw bale, wooden pallet, concrete block, or a three-section compost bin to build it in.

Supplies and tools

- Wood chipper or shredder (rented or borrowed if you do not own one)

- Large supply of hay, leaves, and small sticks

- Alfalfa meal

- Water supply (garden hose)

- Rake (for moving compost materials into place)

- Garden fork or shovel (for turning the pile)

- Compost ingredients (hay, leaves, sticks, any spent garden plants)

- Enough straw bales to make a wall for the front of the bin, plus a few extra bales to cover the top

Instructions

1. Feed a combination of hay, leaves, plants, and sticks through the shredder or chipper, creating enough chips to form a 3- to 4-inch layer in the compost bin. Spread it out evenly with the rake.

2. Sprinkle it generously with the alfalfa meal, and wet the pile with the hose.

3. Repeat the layers until the pile is 18 inches high.

4. Put on a 4- to 6-inch layer of unchopped hay to provide aeration.

5. Repeat layers of brown material, alfalfa meal, and unchopped hay until the pile is about 5 feet high.

6. Stack hay or straw bales along the opening of the bin. Break open some bales and stack the flakes of hay or bunches of straw on top to insulate the compost.

7. Water the entire compost pile.

The pile should begin to warm up within 24 hours. By about the third day it should be hot and ready to turn. Turn the pile with a garden fork every three days for two weeks until the composting action ends and the pile cools.

Sheet Compost

Sheet composting is simple and provides a quick way to get organic matter into the ground at the end of the growing season. Crop remainders, such as corn stalks, bean and pea vines, and other vegetable waste, can be left in the field and used as part of sheet composting. To make sheet compost, spread grass clippings, leaves, meal, or manure on the field, and till it into the soil by hand, with a rototiller, or a tractor with a tiller attachment. Manure or meal may be necessary to provide enough nitrogen to compost the carbon-rich materials. Without the additional nitrogen source, the carbon may use up a lot of the nitrogen in the soil as it composts, making the soil less fertile for the next season's plantings.

Sheet composting is similar to **green manure composting**, which consists of growing and then plowing under nitrogen-rich and nitrogen fixer crops, such as soybean, clover, and alfalfa. A nitrogen fixer is a plant that accumulates large amounts of nitrogen in its roots. If you want to avoid tilling and disturbing the soil, you can mow down the crops and then cover the area with sheets of cardboard or layers of newspaper to kill off the plants. If you do this in the fall, by spring the newspaper will have disintegrated, the plants will have composted in place, and the land will be ready for planting.

Leaf Mold Compost

Leaf mold is essentially rotted leaves and is a valuable addition to the soil. It behaves somewhat like peat and can be used to amend garden soil, as bedding in a worm bin, and as a seed starter. Leaf mold is water-retentive and can absorb up to five times its weight in water. Because leaf mold is so good at retaining water, you can use it as mulch in dry, shady areas, such as under trees. Over time the leaf mold will create soil suitable for growing shade-loving plants. It contains few, if any, weed seeds. Because it is low in nutrients, you should mix it with blood, fish, bone, hoof, horn, or seaweed meal to provide nutrients to the seeds and seedlings beyond their first few days. You can also make an excellent seed starter by mixing one part leaf mold with one part sifted compost or worm castings.

To make leaf mold, simply pile up dry leaves, stomp on them to break them up a bit, water the pile, and leave it alone. In about two years, you will have leaf mold. To create leaf mold more quickly, shred the leaves, use a soaker hose to keep the pile wet, chop through the leaf pile with a sharp hoe or mattock, or stir in green materials, such as wet coffee grounds, alfalfa meal, or fresh grass clippings. You can also speed the process by mixing five parts leaves with one part manure. The leaves will break down four or five times as fast as if they were just piled up. You can also create a peat substitute by layering leaves with grass and letting it slowly decay into leaf mold.

Dried decaying leaves.

CASE STUDY

John Cossham
Amateur composter
York, United Kingdom
http://lowcarbonlifestyle.
blogspot.com/

"I have a large garden, 80 meters long by 7 meters wide (about 262 feet by 23 feet), and I currently have more than 40 composting systems in it. I am a 'deep green.' Someone who claims to be green is keen on the environment, but there are different levels of commitment. If you are 'light green,' you do not take it very seriously, but if you are a 'deep green,' you live your whole life according to ecological principles, are extremely aware of all the issues, and are not at all hypocritical regarding your beliefs and your actions. I am extremely passionate and driven to live a low-carbon lifestyle, and I try to make everything I do as low impact and positive as possible. I was featured on BBC Newsnight's *Ethical Man* television show **http://news.bbc.co.uk/1/hi/programmes/newsnight/7510447.stm**.

I am especially interested in waste issues and use my garden to divert materials destined for the landfill by composting them and keeping the material in the living environment. I collect from a greengrocer, a supermarket, and a café with my bicycle trailer and bring in more than 100 kilograms (about 220 pounds) of material every week.

I have two wood stoves, and the hedges and sawdust from my logging operations give me plenty of carbon-rich material to balance the mainly green/sappy fruit and vegetable material I bring in. I also have a home-made compost toilet, which means I am not wasting water. The finished compost is mostly given away or sold for a donation, used in the garden, and used to make growing media for pots in the conservatory, where we grow tomatoes, cucumbers, peppers, yams, and such. I use my garden as a demonstration garden so people can see the different compost systems available, and I also test different compost bins and tumblers as part of my York Rotters work. (The York Rotters are a network of volunteers in York, U.K., who provide advice and support to composters.)

I have a large selection of different bins, tumblers, wormeries, and other types of composting systems.

- Four wormeries
- Five working tumblers
- 15 Daleks with compost, one with sawdust, one with leaf mold, two with loam
- Two ex-tumblers
- One fabric bin
- One green cone
- Six New Zealand bins
- One leaf mold enclosure
- One Komp 700
- One air-raid shelter bin
- Two radiator beds (not currently being used for composting)
- Seven builders' bags

This makes 41 active compost bins / wormeries and a handful of storage containers and others. I am currently testing a CompoSphere for York Rotters. (A **CompoSphere** is a spherical compost container that can be rolled like a ball to mix the contents.)

I have been fascinated by decomposition since childhood, when I remember putting assorted objects into jars to watch them go moldy on my windowsill. I did my dissertation for my environmental health degree on local authority composting. I love nature and love the life associated with my many compost heaps. I hate waste and love recycling. I know that organic materials in landfills release carbon in the form of methane, a greenhouse gas 23 times more powerful than carbon dioxide, whereas if aerobically composted, some carbon is emitted as CO_2, and lots of carbon is kept as humus and can be sequestered in soil by top-dressing. I get a thrill from creating 'something for nothing.' I have Asperger's Syndrome and am a bit obsessive compulsive, and I am very driven to be low carbon, ethical, and green. I really love composting.

I enjoy all aspects of composting: waste reduction, hot heaps, cold heaps, digging out, sifting, sales/donating, worms, wildlife, teaching kids, teaching adults, meeting other composters, volunteering with York

Rotters, answering questions on Facebook and assorted fora, everything. The only part of composting that I dislike is not having enough time for it, finding a sack of stuff I should have put on the current heap and having to sort it out when it is half decomposed and a bit messy, and dealing with authorities and organizations that sometimes make life more complicated than I'd like.

I discovered *The Humanure Handbook* by Joe Jenkins in 2002 and immediately installed my own composting toilet (a commode, brewing bucket, bag of partly composted sawdust), and then when the television show *Ethical Man* came on and asked, "What should I do and not do?" I e-mailed in and mentioned the compost loo. [Author's note: *Ethical Man* is a BBC television series about a journalist who tried for one year to live as ethically as possible. This included going without a car, recycling and composting as much as possible, and interviewing many people who are living green lifestyles. The series is continuing with *Ethical Man* traveling to the United States.]

He e-mailed back and asked if he could come and film it. I said, 'Of course,' and that was the start of an amazing lot of TV appearances, writing a column for a national magazine, and most recently, being invited to become a Fellow of the Royal Society for the encouragement of Arts, Manufactures and Commerce (RSA), so I will be able to call myself John Cossham FRSA. (This is not just for composting. I founded North Yorkshire Credit Union and York Green Festival, as well as York Rotters.) Who knows what will happen next?

CHAPTER 6

MAINTAINING A COMPOST BIN

> *"It is only when you start a garden — probably after age 50 — that you realize something important happens every day."*
>
> — Geoffrey B. Charlesworth, author

Composting will take place in any pile of debris whether there is human intervention or not. But if you want to produce compost to use in your garden, chances are you do not want to wait for years for things to decay on their own. Properly maintaining your compost pile helps speed the composting process and creates healthier compost. Maintaining a compost pile mainly requires feeding it correct amounts of green and brown waste and making sure it has adequate water and air. Depending on the kind of compost pile or bin you use, you will need different tools to stir, turn, or aerate it.

Aerating a Stationary Bin

You can aerate a stationary bin with an aerating tool. These are long metal stakes with either a screw-shaped end (like an auger), or a spring-loaded end that enters the compost smoothly and then pops open little wing-like extensions when you pull back on it. To "turn" the compost in a stationary bin, you simply twist or poke the tool down into the bottom of the compost bin and pull it back out several times. This pokes holes down through the layers and lets oxygen get in. You can also insert pipes with holes drilled in them when you create the pile. You can let these pipes stick out of the pile, or can lay them on the ground and build the pile on top of them with the ends of the pipes extending outside the pile. This will allow some air to flow down into the pile, but it may require additional turning to get enough oxygen into the mixture.

Aerating an Outdoor Bin or Heap

Some gardeners worry about turning an outdoor compost pile too often, fearing that the cooling that happens during the turning process will slow decomposition. However, this fear is unfounded because turning the undigested matter to the inside of the compost heap after the initial heating and cooling period will almost immediately put the microbes back to work consuming this fresh food. A well-fed and properly sized pile should heat up again in a day or two, and the small loss of heat is more than made up for when fresh air is introduced into the pile, energizing the aerobic bacteria. Just be sure not to turn the pile while it is at its warmest, since this will interrupt the composting process.

The following are ways you can turn compost in various types of compost containers:

- If you decide to use a wire bin, you can pick it up and move it aside. Once you are done, you can fork the contents back into the bin.

- If you decide to compost in a trash bag, you can shake the bag every day and open it only when you want to add more material.

- Tumbling bins are turned without losing heat because the contents are not exposed to the air; you simply rotate the drum and the compost is mixed. Air enters through the holes in the bin and aerates the compost.

- A three-bin system is turned by forking or shoveling the contents from the last bin (that should now be finished compost) into a wheelbarrow or other container for use. The contents of the middle bin are then forked into the last bin, and the contents of the first bin are forked into the center, freeing up the first bin to be filled with fresh material.

Using a pitchfork to turn the composting material.

Compost should be turned when it starts to cool down, usually a few days after building the initial pile. If it is too wet or smelly, you should turn it every day until it dries out. You can also add dry, brown materials when you turn a wet pile to soak up the excess liquid and provide additional carbon, which will even out the balance. If you have a slow or medium compost pile, you can turn it less often — every couple of weeks for a medium pile or once every month or two for a slow pile.

If you want to be thorough and turn the pile according to temperature, you can purchase compost thermometers. These are made especially for compost piles and are covered in metal to prevent breakage. They range in size from 18 to 30 inches long and have a digital or analog readout on the top. They range in price from about $15 to $30. An inexpensive oven thermometer will also work and can be buried in the middle of the pile. Consider tying colorful yarn to the thermometer so you will be less likely to lose it in the pile. You can test the temperature by feel if you are experienced, but if your pile is very hot, you risk scalding yourself if you stick your hand into the middle of the pile.

Watering

Water is a vital element in the compost pile. Even enclosed bins sometimes need to be watered if they contain too much brown, carbon-rich material and not enough green, wet material. Water helps to break down some of the materials in the compost, it feeds the microbes and larger creatures in the pile, and it protects the pile from some pests you may not want, such as ants, which prefer dry piles.

If you have an open compost pile, it will get rained on, but if you live in a dry climate or have a cover on your pile, you will have to water it yourself. You can use collected rainwater, water from a garden hose, or ordinary tap water. If you want to use watering as an opportunity to add more nutrients to the pile, save water left over from cooking vegetables or pasta. As long as this water does not contain oils or butter, you can pour it directly onto the compost. Some composters also collect and dilute their urine to give their compost a nitrogen boost.

The optimal moisture level for a compost pile or bin is 45 to 50 percent. You can determine the moisture level by squeezing a

Moisture meter.

handful of compost. If a few drops of water come out, then the moisture is at the right level. If you want a less hands-on and more accurate method for determining moisture content, purchase a moisture meter.

If your compost pile gets too wet, several problems may occur. Nutrients may leach out of the compost and into the surrounding soil, wasting your efforts. The aerobic bacteria in the pile also may drown. This is more common in enclosed plastic bins, because in an open pile the water will drain away (unless your land is completely flooded). In a bin, the water often has nowhere to go, and you will end up with compost soup. Stationary bins with drain holes in the bottom help alleviate this problem, but nutrients will still leach out.

If compost is only slightly wet, try adding more brown materials, especially items like shredded paper or cardboard that will absorb the water. You can also fork or turn the compost or even spread it out on the ground to dry. You will lose any heat that has built up, and will have to start over, but that is preferable to throwing out a whole batch of half-made compost.

To keep an outdoor compost pile from getting too wet in the first place, always build it on well-drained ground. If you are using a bin, make sure it has some kind of drainage holes. (This is especially vital for vermicompost bins.) Enclosed bins should have lids that direct water away from the enclosure. If you have an open compost pile (either enclosed or piled up in the open), you can cover it with a tarp during heavy rain. Remember to remove the tarp when the rain stops so that mold and mildew will not grow in the pile.

When is Compost Ready to Use?

Compost is "done" or mature and ready to use when it smells like fresh, clean earth. It is crumbly, dark brown, and slightly moist, and the compost pile is the same temperature as the surrounding air, meaning that many of the bacteria have stopped eating and respiring. Finished compost may still have about 25 or 30 percent organic material in it, and even at this stage, compost will continue to decompose for up to two years.

Your climate will affect how long it will take your compost to be fully ready for use (in hot climates, it may take a shorter period of time and in cooler climates it may take longer). The way your compost was built and maintained will also play a factor in the amount of time before your compost can be added to your garden.

At this point, you should cure the compost by letting it sit for six to 12 weeks. During this time, organic acids will dissipate; the particles will shrink as they lose moisture and will become more uniform; the amount of nitrogen will actually increase; and the pH will stabilize and move closer to the neutral range. During the curing stage, you should keep the compost off the ground to avoid infiltration by roots. You may want to spread it on a tarp or piece of burlap. Keep it slightly damp and poke it with a digging fork from time to time to let air get down into it. There is no need to turn curing compost. You can also cure compost in a closed bin, but you should open it to allow for ventilation every few days at the beginning and then every few weeks as it matures. You should also spray it lightly with water to keep it just slightly damp.

If you are not sure your compost is complete, you can test it by mixing a small amount with potting soil and planting some lettuce seeds. Plant the same type of seeds in plain potting soil and watch the plants as they sprout and grow. The seeds in the compost mixture should grow as well as, or better than, those in the plain potting soil. If not, let your compost mature further.

Jeff raking out compost for use in the garden. Courtesy of Karen Gault.

CASE STUDY

Robert and Debra Post
Amateur composters
Fort Payne, Alabama

"We compost for the same reason we recycle: to reduce the flow into landfills. For us, the most enjoyable aspect of composting is taking sustenance from the earth and returning it to the earth. There is nothing unpleasant about composting. Waiting for the vegetable scraps to convert to compost is the only hard part. After harvest, we work the compost into the garden soil. In flower beds, we also work it into the soil when mulching or when preparing new beds.

At our previous home, we had an open compost bin far from our house, near the woods and a small stream. It was interesting to see the little footprints and sparking clean eggshells. A few months later, we saw baby skunks in the yard. There is no way we can be sure the skunks cleaned the eggshells, but it was nice to have them around to remove grubs from the lawn. Our little 'ecology' paid dividends in the form of a smooth, mole-free yard. When the grubs were gone, the moles left too.

We do not do any indoor composting because we have limited space inside, but lots of room outside. We have not tried vermicomposting, but Debbie conducted experiments with leaves and worms in college. It was amazing to see how much the worms consumed in such a short time.

To make our compost, we use a homemade barrel and fill it with fruit and vegetable scraps, eggshells, and coffee grounds. We enjoy building the equipment ourselves and would be happy to share our plans for the barrel composter. It is just one more piece of our nature conservation and money-saving techniques along with recycling and rainwater collection. It is so simple anyone can do it."

CHAPTER 7

USING COMPOST

Compost is most useful when it has completely finished maturing, but it can also be used when it is slightly underdone. Compost that is not quite ready for use may still have some undigested bits of plant, fruit, or vegetable matter in it. The bits may or may not be recognizable as food. It will not have the characteristic look and may not have the clean, rich smell of finished compost. It may still be warm to the touch because the microorganisms are still living and working in it. It should be mostly dark brown in color.

When you use it depends on what you are using it for and where and how you plan to use it. Compost should be sifted before use to remove any large pieces, because these pieces are not finished breaking down. *This sifting process is described later in this chapter.* Return these pieces to the compost to finish decaying. Compost materials that have not fully decayed will finish composting in or on the ground, but if they are dug or tilled into the soil, they can use up available nitrogen as they decompose. This will rob nitrogen from your plants, and so it is better to let the compost mature fully or to use unfinished compost only as mulch. If unfinished compost is used as mulch, it will leach nutrients slowly into the soil, giving your plants a constant supply of nutrients over a period of weeks rather than one big boost of energy.

Finished compost should be used as soon as possible because letting it sit will cause it to leach nutrients back into the air and soil. The fibers and aggregate clumps will break down into smaller and smaller pieces, and soon it will lose its soil-amending quali-

Jeff using the rich moist compost ready for the garden. Courtesy of Karen Gault.

ties. It should sit for no longer than six months before use. It is better to use compost that is not quite mature than to leave it sitting around for too long.

Where to Use Compost

Compost can be used everywhere in the garden. It adds beneficial microbes to the soil, retains water, and suppresses weeds and many plant diseases. Compost works best if you apply it after a rain, or after watering the garden, is not, or lawn. The following are some ways and places you can use your compost:

- To feed new lawns, spread a layer of compost ¼-inch deep over the grass seed.

- To dress bare spots on lawns, spread a dense layer of compost on the bare spots.

- Use compost as mulch in vegetable and flower gardens. Make sure to use only mature, sifted compost around new plantings to avoid damage from undigested organic material and weed seeds.

- Use sifted compost as a seed starter in a one-to-one combination with either leaf mold or worm castings.

- Use sifted compost as bedding in a worm bin by mixing it one-to-one with damp, shredded newspaper.

- Use a combination of one-third compost and two-thirds potting soil in flowerpots and containers. Soil is necessary to give the plant roots something to grip, so do not plant them in 100-percent compost.

- Use compost on sandy or clay soils to amend them by re-taining moisture, improving drainage, and introducing beneficial bacteria.

- Use compost around trees of any age to suppress weeds, prevent erosion, and protect from drought. Spread a 2- to 4-inch layer out to the drip line of the tree twice a year. (The drip line is an imaginary circle around the tree just under the tips of the branches.)

Healthy Soil Leads to Healthy Produce

Small, young tomato bush growing in compost.

Decades of commercial farming with the use of artificially produced fertilizers have left many soils depleted of nutrients. A University of Illinois study looked at soil samples collected over the past 100 years from the Morrow Plots — the oldest experimental field in the United States. They discovered that yields were 20 percent lower in the portion of the field that received the most fertilization with synthetic nitrogen fertilizers. They analyzed soil samples and found that there had been an average decrease in soil organic carbon of 4.9 tons per acre. Over-fertilization with artificial nitrogen fertilizers leads to a loss of carbon in the soil, which in turn decreases soil's ability to store water. While synthetic fertilizer is important, the scientists pointed out that "excessive application rates cut profits and are bad for soils and the environment."

If there are fewer nutrients in the soil, there will be fewer nutrients in the fruits and vegetables we grow and, therefore, in our diets. Studies conducted on commercially grown produce in the United States, United Kingdom, and Canada have all shown marked decreases in vitamins and minerals in common foods grown since 1951.

Information in the table below was taken from data gathered and analyzed in 2002 for CTV News, a Canadian news network. It shows the percentage change in common vitamins and nutrients in selected produce grown between 1951 and 1999. Negative changes are noted, and, as you can see, with the single exception of corn, all of these common foods now have much smaller quantities of several important nutrients than they did just a few decades ago.

	Calcium	Iron	Vitamin A	Vitamin C	Thiamin	Ribo-flavin	Niacin
Apples	20.00	-53.33	-41.11	16.00	-75.00	-66.67	-30.00
Bananas	-23.75	-41.67	-81.16	-13.00	0.00	100.00	-1.43
Blueberries	-59.38	-83.75	-64.25	-30.00	160.00	160.00	-30.00
Broccoli	-62.85	-33.85	-55.94	-10.10	-40.00	-42.86	-2.73
Carrots	-29.49	-37.50	135.88	46.67	66.67	0.00	126.00
Cauliflower	-1.36	-57.27	-79.00	-33.04	-45.45	-30.00	56.67
Celery	-20.00	0.00	-86.50	7.14	0.00	25.00	25.00
Cherries	-18.33	10.25	-65.38	-8.13	-11.80	0.00	47.00
Corn	35.00	12.50	60.00	8.00	125.00	80.00	60.00
Cranberries	-42.86	-66.67	15.00	0.00	33.33	0.00	100.00
Cucumbers	36.50	-10.00	n/a	-31.75	0.00	-50.00	35.00
Grapes	-29.41	-66.67	-10.00	150.00	66.67	50.00	100.00

	Calcium	Iron	Vitamin A	Vitamin C	Thiamin	Ribo-flavin	Niacin
Green Peppers	16.82	22.50	0.31	-25.83	75.00	-57.14	67.50
Lettuce (iceberg)	-13.64	0.00	-38.89	-34.00	25.00	-62.50	50.00
Onions	-37.31	-52.80	-100.0	-54.62	57.33	-41.00	136.00
Oranges	19.70	-80.00	-89.26	8.57	0.00	0.00	150.00
Peaches	-42.50	-83.33	-96.21	0.00	-75.00	25.00	11.11
Peas	-37.56	-52.43	14.31	11.00	0.00	29.50	22.10
Pears	-13.85	52.50	0.00	2.50	-50.00	0.00	100.00
Potatoes	-27.55	-57.14	-100	-57.35	-18.18	-50.00	45.00
Red Peppers	-16.82	22.50	185.10	52.00	0.00	-25.00	67.50
Spinach	23.10	-9.87	-28.72	-51.31	-23.18	-7.05	125.33
Squash	-58.82	-33.33	-27.63	16.25	60.00	-75.00	86.00
Strawberries	-52.50	-62.50	-55.50	-5.00	-33.33	0.00	0.00
Tomatoes	-55.64	-18.33	-43.36	-1.58	0.00	25.00	46.00

Because compost contains a wider variety of nutrients than commercial fertilizers, and because it has soil-amending qualities that help oxygen and water get to plant roots, it does a great job at making your vegetable plants more vigorous and healthy. If you want to feed yourself and your family a healthy diet, growing your own produce and feeding it with compost will go a long way toward ensuring your family receives all the vitamins and minerals they need.

Preparing Compost for Use

Before you can use your compost, you will need to transform it into a usable state. If you are just mulching with it, you can spread the compost directly from the compost pile once it has finished decaying. But if you plan to use it in containers, flowerpots, as a seed starter, or around new plantings, you will have to sift it. *Instructions for making a compost sifter are included below.* You may also want to make compost tea to water both indoor and outdoor plants. *Instructions for making compost tea are included later in this chapter.* Before you use compost, you may want to check your soil condition. Determining the soil pH and learning what minerals it lacks will help you decide where to use compost to its best advantage.

Testing for pH levels

Finished compost should have a neutral pH, meaning it is neither acidic nor alkaline. The pH scale ranges from 1 — very acidic — to 14 — very alkaline — so neutral soil or compost will have a pH level of 7. Most plants flourish best in the range of 6 to 7 on the pH scale because it is at this range that most of the important nutrients, including nitrogen, phosphorus, and potassium, are available to the plant. For this reason, compost can be used everywhere in your garden without harming plants. Also, because it is neutral, it will not burn your plants the way fresh manure or synthetic fertilizers might.

If you have used an overabundance of acidic materials, such as pine needles, pine sawdust, or oak leaves in your compost, you should let the compost mature completely before using it. As leaves and evergreen needles decompose, their pH level rises, making these plant items less acidic and almost neutral.

You should do a pH test of the soil in your lawn or garden to determine what kind of amendments it may need. You may want to check each flower bed or garden plot individually because pH can vary widely even in the same area. Knowing the pH of the soil in different planting beds, garden areas, and containers will help you customize the soil environment to the needs of your plants and will result in stronger, healthier vegetation.

Whether your garden soil is acidic or alkaline, adding compost will help bring it back into neutral territory. This is desirable for most plants, but some, such as azaleas, rhododendrons, and hydrangeas, love acidic soil. For plants like these, you may want to amend the compost-enriched soil with extra helpings of acidic materials such as pine needles. Hydrangeas, in particular, are very responsive to soil pH and the color of the flowers varies with the pH. In a low pH soil of about 5 to 5.5, the flowers will be blue. A pH level of 6 or higher will produce pink flowers. To find out what kind of soil is best for your plants, check with a local greenhouse or your nearest university extension office.

To test your soil pH, you can use a simple kit from a garden store or local extension service. These kits range in price from about $1 for a single-use kit, to hundreds of dollars for professional test kits. A mid-range kit of $10 or $20 is adequate for almost any household garden. Most kits include enough supplies to test dozens of samples, so you can test individual flower beds or vegetable plots easily. The mid-range and high-end kits will also tell you the levels of nitrogen, phosphorus, and potassium in the soil, so you can amend if necessary. Truly dedicated gardeners might want to purchase a pH meter. This device has a probe that you insert into damp earth, and after a minute, it gives you the pH of that particular area. These devices cost about $25 and are available at most garden supply stores or online.

Testing is easy, and instructions will come with any test kit you purchase. In general, you should collect a soil sample from 2 to 3 inches below the surface. Mix the soil with the specified amount of water and shake the mixture in the container provided. Add the chemical that came with the kit, wait the required length of time, then read the color-coded results on the container to see your pH level. Sometimes you will discover that your soil pH is just fine. If not, the test kit should contain a chart that will tell you how much lime (in the form of ground limestone) to add to make the soil more alkaline, or how much sulphur to add to make it more acidic. You can purchase either of these materials at a gardening supply store or online.

Keep in mind that lime does not work immediately. It can take a few months for the lime to fully integrate with the soil. Also, applying lime while plants are growing can be harmful to the plants, so it is best to treat the soil in the fall or the very early spring to give the lime a chance to work. The rule of thumb among gardeners is to sprinkle enough limestone on the garden so that it looks like a light snowfall, or like the powdered sugar on a doughnut. If you add lime to your garden in the fall, test the pH again in the early spring to see if the soil is now in the range you need it to be. If not, you may want to treat it again with another light application. Rake the limestone into the surface and water it. If you are liming early in the spring and your area gets rain, it may be enough to let the spring rains soak the lime into the soil.

Sulphur also does not work instantly. Microbes in the soil break down sulphur into sulfate, and this can take several months. Because sulphur relies on living creatures for this transformation, you should apply it in the spring when soil microbes will be active. The amount of sulphur you add will depend on the composition of your soil. If it has more sand, more silt, or more clay, the amounts you have to add will differ. If the soil contains a lot of calcium carbonate, you will need additional sulphur to decrease the pH. Detailed instructions for determining how much sulphur to add can be found in this fact sheet produced by the Ohio State University Extension: **http://ohioline.osu.edu/ agf-fact/pdf/0507.pdf**.

Now that you have tested your soil and know where you want to put your compost, you can prepare the compost for use by sifting it. This step is important because it will remove large, undecayed pieces of compost and will give you a uniform product to work with.

Making a Compost Sifter

Even matured compost can sometimes be too coarse to use right out of the bin or pile. If you plan to use compost in containers, as a growing medium for new seedlings, or around flower beds or delicate vegetables, you will have to screen out the larger pieces. The simplest way to screen compost is in a **compost sifter**, which is a wooden box with a metal screen attached to the bottom. Simply put handfuls of compost into the sifter, and shake it lightly from side to side. The finished compost will pass through the screen and the large, uncomposted pieces will remain so you can return them to the bin where they can decompose further. Here are instructions for making a simple compost sifter. You can alter the dimensions if you want a bigger or smaller one — for example, if you want to make one that exactly fits over your wheelbarrow. These instructions were adapted from the book, *Basic Composting*.

Supplies and tools

- One 1x6, 8 feet long

- 18-inch x 24-inch piece of ½-inch wire mesh (hardware cloth)

- 12 2-inch galvanized deck screws

- Four 1 ⅝-inch galvanized deck screws

- Hammer

- Wire clippers

- Staple gun and ½-inch staples

- Drill with ⅛-inch bit, Phillips screwdriver bit, and countersink bit

- Crosscut saw or circular saw

- Two sawhorses

- Carpenter's square

- Tape measure

- Coarse sand paper

- Pencil

Instructions

Measuring

1. Measure an 18-inch by 24-inch rectangle of hardware cloth and cut with the wire clippers.

2. Measure and mark a ⅜-inch line along the full length of the 1x6 board.

3. Measure and mark two 17-inch lengths and two 24 ½-inch lengths on the board.

Cutting

4. Support the board on two sawhorses and use the circular saw (or hand saw) to cut the ⅜-inch strip off the edge of the board. If you find it difficult to make such a long straight cut, try cutting along the marks made in Step 3

before cutting the ⅜-inch strip off. That way you can make four shorter cuts, which may be more accurate.

5. Cut the strip into four sections on the marks made in Step 3.

6. Cut the remaining board into four sections on the marks made in Step 3.

Marking and Drilling

7. Mark drilling holes ⅜ inch from each end of each of the 24 ½-inch boards as follows: one hole in the center and the other two ¾ inch from each long edge as shown below. In the diagram below, the width of the board in the diagram is shown as 5 ⅝ inch because ⅜ inch was removed in Step 4. This is an approximation because 1x6s are not really a full 6 inches wide.

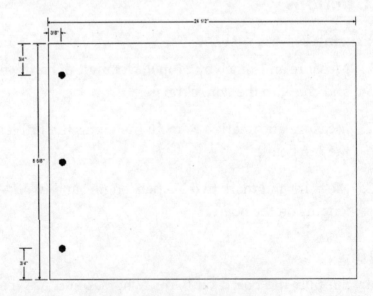

8. Using the ¹/₈-inch drill bit, drill the marked holes on each end of each of the 24 ½-inch boards.

9. On each ⅜-inch wood strip, mark, and drill holes ¾ inch from both ends and about every 4 inches in between as shown below. Diagram is not to scale.

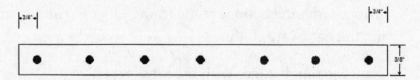

10. Using the countersink bit, countersink all the drilled holes deep enough to accommodate the head of the deck screws.

Assembling

11. Using the 12 2-inch deck screws and the Phillips screw-driver bit, attach the 24½-inch boards to the 17-inch boards to form a rectangle, placing the longer boards outside the shorter ones as shown below and using three screws on each corner. Use the carpenter's square to ensure the rect-angle is square as you assemble it.

12. Use the staple gun to attach the hardware cloth to the frame, stapling about every 3 inches around the frame.

13. Use the hammer to ensure the staples are secure in the wood frame.

14. Using the 1 ⅝-inch deck screws, attach the ⅜-inch wood strip around the bottom of the frame, covering and securing the hardware cloth.

15. Sand the rough edges with the sand paper.

Using

To use your screen, place it over a wheelbarrow or large container and pour in finished compost, about 1 gallon at a time, shaking the screen from side to side to let the finished compost fall through the holes. Return any large pieces back to the compost bin.

Making Compost Tea

Compost tea is a solution made of finished compost and water. Just like compost, it is full of healthy microbes and nutrients, and because it is in a liquid form, plants can absorb it quickly. Compost tea can be aerated using aquarium pumps and other means. **Aeration** is the process of introducing air into the tea, which helps keep the microbes in it alive so that they can reproduce. Vigorously stirring the tea daily will also help incorporate some air into the mixture without the trouble and expense of pumps, but it is not as efficient at aerating the water.

Supplies and Tools

- 5-gallon bucket

- Burlap bag or other cloth sack

- Short length of rope, such as hay rope

- Rocks (to weigh the sack down)

- Fish tank bubbler or aerator

Instructions

1. Fill a burlap bag with finished compost. Tie the top shut. As with any kind of tea, adding more of the active ingredient — in this case compost — will make the tea stronger, but to make 5 gallons of tea, about 1 gallon of compost should be enough.

2. Put the bag into the 5-gallon bucket, and weight it down with rocks if necessary.

3. Fill the container with water (the ratio should be about five parts water to one part compost), and let the compost soak for several days, stirring it at least once a day to aerate it. You can also aerate it using a fish tank aerator or bubbler. You can use an external pump with a long hose leading into the bottom of compost tea bucket or a submersible aerator attached to the side of the bucket with one or more hoses extending down into the tea. Whichever kind you choose, make sure to follow all safety instructions that come with the aerator.

4. Remove the bag and squeeze the excess water out of the bag. You can re-use the bag several times. If you do not plan to make additional compost tea, you may take the compost that was in the bag and add it to the garden or back into the compost pile if it is not done composting.

5. Check that the compost tea is good to use. It should smell earthy and fresh. If it smells like sulfur or smells sour or spoiled, do not use it. Instead, pour it back onto the com-

post pile and try again with different compost. The sour smell comes from anaerobic bacteria, which can be discouraged by frequent stirring or mechanical aeration.

How to use compost tea

1. Strain out any large bits of compost material that may have escaped the bag. You can do this by using a few layers of cheesecloth stretched over a second bucket or by using a small fish net to scoop out visible pieces.

2. Dilute the tea — ten parts water to one part tea.

3. Use compost tea to water plants every one to two weeks.

4. You can also use the tea as a foliar fertilizer by spraying the tops and bottoms of leaves. (A **foliar fertilizer** is one that is sprayed directly onto the foliage — leaves and stems — rather than on the soil.) To help the tea adhere to the leaves, you may add one drop of clear liquid soap (not detergent and not an anti-bacterial formula) to the mixture. The soap will allow the liquid to spread smoothly over the leaves instead of forming droplets. This helps the tea stick to the leaves. If you do not want to spray soap on food crops, you can find various organic products that can accomplish the same task for sale at gardening supply stores or online. These products are called **surfactants,** and they help the compost tea, pesticides, and other liquid sprays cling to the leaves by breaking the surface tension of the liquid. This causes the liquid to form a sheet over the leaves rather than forming little droplets that are not as effective at transferring their ingredients to the plant.

5. Spray plants with a fine mist in the morning or evening when it is cool (below 72 degrees), not during periods of

bright sunlight or when temperatures are over 80 degrees. When it is cool, the pores on the leaves are open and the fertilizer can penetrate the leaves more easily.

Although it seems to take a long time to make compost, once you start, you will have a continuous supply for as long as you keep doing it. Getting to the point of sifting it, making tea from it, and applying it to the garden provides a great feeling of accomplishment, but it is still just part of the ongoing cycle. The plants you feed today will turn into the compost materials you will pile up this fall so that the cycle may continue.

CASE STUDY

Marianne Carlson
Amateur composter
Fort Dodge, Iowa

My compost system consists of a plastic ice cream bucket under the sink. When that gets full, I put it in a chicken-wire compost bin outside and turn the compost with a potato fork. Compost is a beautiful, rich material. It is wonderful. The worms you get in there are huge. Fishermen ought to do this.

I started to compost because I had a lot of yard waste, and waste from salads, vegetables, and canning, such as skins from tomatoes and peppers. We eat a lot of salads at our house. Start eating the way you are supposed to — eat your vegetables — and composting just comes naturally. If you want to spend $50, you can buy a fancy unit for your counter, but it does not have to be complicated.

I do not always follow the rules. They say compost has to be a certain temperature, and that you have to let it get hot enough to kill all the seeds and germs. In my case that does not always happen. I have had decorative gourds growing out of my compost pile, miniature white pumpkins, and cannas. I had thrown away some canna bulbs; I thought they were dead, but they were not. They stayed warm enough in there over the winter, and they sprouted. And apparently, with my gourds and pumpkins, it was not hot enough to kill the seeds, which was a plus as far as I was concerned. It is right by my rhubarb patch, which loves the compost. Rhubarb is a heavy eater.

I compost grass clippings, although you should not use them if you treat your yard, and you do not want too many grass clippings because that becomes overwhelming. I also compost kitchen scraps, yard waste, squash peelings, apple cores, and banana peels. Do not compost meat, bones, or anything similar, or you are asking for trouble from critters.

Composting can be as much or as little work as you want. I like having it in three stages: the first, where the ingredients are all piled up and mixed together; the second stage, where it is brewed awhile; and the third, where it is ready to be used. You can get real complicated as far as having air space underneath, but that is not for me. I just do it my way. I make it up as I go along.

The only problems I have experienced are with grass clippings. Make sure you do not have too many because they become rancid very quickly. That was the only problem I have ever had.

The most important thing about composting is that it is one less thing that goes to the city dump. They do not have to pick up many bags of garbage at my house. So, that is a plus; it keeps it out of the landfill. It is a plus for your yard, and it is good for some of the critters over the winter. Sometimes the birds and rabbits will feed on the compost. I do not spend much on soil enrichment materials. What I like about compost is what it does to your soil.

CHAPTER 8

VERMICOMPOSTING

"... cabbage leaves and pieces of onion were ... devoured with much relish by worms ... Judging by their eagerness for certain kinds of food, they must enjoy the pleasure of eating."

— Charles Darwin

Vermicomposting is the process of using worms to help break down the organic matter in a compost pile or bin. If your outdoor compost pile sits directly on the soil, there will most likely be worms in it when it is cool enough for them to survive. They will use the pile for food and shelter, appreciating the dampness in the heat of summer and relative warmth in the cold of winter. Worms will burrow away if the pile gets too hot for them, but often return when the pile cools down.

You can practice vermicomposting indoors or outdoors, and it is an ideal composting system if you do not have a yard or cannot manage outdoor compost systems. Even if you have an outdoor system, you can use vermicomposting so that your cooked food scraps do not go to waste. Castings from vermicomposting help many plant species, and some, such as carrots, cucumbers, tomatoes, peppers, corn, grapes, strawberries, and marigolds, do especially well in casting-enriched soil.

VERMICOMPOSTING — A GREAT WAY TO GET KIDS INVOLVED!

Kids love playing in the dirt and love learning how things work. Teaching them about composting with worms is a great way to encourage their love of nature and to get them involved in creating a healthier environment for their own future.

- Children can help make bedding for the worms by sifting finished compost or by shredding newspaper. (If you are using an electric paper shredder, be sure to provide adult supervision. Tearing the paper into small strips will work just as well.)

- Determining the right size of worm bin to use involves weighing family food scraps for a week and doing some simple calculations to determine how many worms you need in the bin. Once you know how many worms you need, you will know how large your bin has to be. This is a great way to show kids that math and geometry have practical applications.

| Pounds of food scraps per week | X 2 = | Pounds of worms needed in compost bin |

> • Kids can help deliver the worms to their new home and can help feed them and collect the castings. They may even want to make worm-casting tea to water the garden plants or their own houseplants. *(See the instructions for making worm tea later in this chapter.)*
>
> A worm bin can make a great show-and-tell project for younger children and can even make a nice science fair project for older ones. If you are a teacher and would like some free worm composting-related curriculum materials, check out The California Education and the Environment Initiative **www.calrecycle. ca.gov/Education/Curriculum**. This website offers educational information and ideas to help children of all ages learn about composting. They also offer a vermicomposting guide for teachers with information on how to start and run a worm bin in your classroom: **www.calrecycle.ca.gov/Education/ Curriculum/Worms.**

Worms — Nature's Own Compost Machine

Worms live in the soil all over the world except in very cold polar regions. They move by expanding and contracting muscles that run down their sides and search through their underground habitat for food. For many years people thought that worms served no useful purpose or were actually harmful to plant roots. In fact, people used to try to kill worms they found in their gardens. In the early 1800s, Charles Darwin began a series of observations and experiments with worms to learn more about them. He even did some early experiments in vermicomposting (although he did not call it that) by burying parts of vegetables and bits of meat in pots of earth containing worms. He then dug up the pots days later to find that the food had been consumed. In 1881, he published a book called *The Formation of Vegetable Mould through the Action of Worms* that described the habits of worms and extolled their virtues for making soil more fertile. Farmers who did not already know that the digging action of worms tilled the soil became fans of worms, but eventually that admiration waned when synthetic fertilizers and mechanical ploughs became more common and widespread. But as Darwin pointed out, having worms in your yard is beneficial in a number of ways.

Worms natures own compost machines.

- Some species pull organic material from the surface of the soil down into their burrows that can be several feet deep. They act on the soil physically, pushing and tunneling through it and pushing or dragging plant matter down into the earth. This helps aerate soil and allows water to infiltrate deeply into soil that might otherwise remain compacted.

Use of an indoor worm box. Courtesy of Karen Gault.

- Worm castings are essentially worm manure and contain calcium, iron, phosphorous, and nitrogen. The casting's complex biochemical makeup helps plants in iron-rich soil absorb nitrogen that would otherwise not be available to the plant.

- Worm castings release nitrogen slowly, allowing plants to feed in a consistent manner. This helps some plants, especially carrots, grow straighter roots. Carrots grown in vermicompost have fewer bad-tasting "hair" roots.

- Castings repel worm-like creatures called root-knot nematodes. These are parasitic creatures that cause deformed roots and drain the nutrients out of the plant. They are responsible for up to 5 percent of crop loss globally.

- Worm castings contain anti-fungal chemicals that can help delicate plants, such as strawberries, by killing off fungal spores that often infect the fruit. Use castings in planting holes or till castings into the earth before planting to help combat or prevent fungal diseases in soft fruit.

- Worms are prey for many other insects and animals. While this may sound like a bad thing, it is actually good for your garden. The same insects and animals that prey on worms eat many garden pests such as slugs. If there are enough worms to keep them fed when there are no slugs or other prey, they will stick around, and when their preferred prey arrives in your garden, they will switch gears to eat those creatures instead of your worms.

- Worms, particularly red worms, consume contaminated soils and clean the contaminants out of the ground. They can eat materials that have been saturated with PCBs (Polychlorinated biphenyls), for example. The chemicals are broken down by the worms' digestive tracts, leaving the soil safe. PCBs are man-made organic chemicals that were used in many products such as paint, adhesives, and fire retardants. They are non-flammable, chemically stable, and have a high boiling point. PCBs were banned in the United States in 1979 when it was discovered that they cause cancer and problems in the immune, reproductive, nervous, and endocrine system. They still exist in the environment and can be released by accident from toxic waste sites.

As you can see, worms not only produce castings, but they also perform a wide variety of helpful tasks that improve the soil, keep plants healthy, and clean up toxins. They are a vital and valuable part of our ecosystem.

Use of an indoor worm box, Courtesy of Karen Gault.

Worm physiology

Worms thrive in the same pH range as most plants (a neutral 6 or 7). They find and identify edible items with the help of special cells surrounding their mouths. These cells can detect a variety of edible chemicals in their environment. Worms can only ingest very small particles and rely on bacteria to break large pieces of food down into small, manageable portions. Worms pull particles of food down into their crop for temporary storage. A **crop** is an enlarged portion of the gullet that exists in birds and some insects. Because they have no teeth, worms grind food in their gizzard in much the same way that birds do. To do this, worms need a source of grit as described a bit later in this chapter.

Worms are hermaphroditic (meaning they have both male and female sex organs), but they cannot reproduce on their own. Instead, they partner and exchange genetic material in the form of secretions from the clitellum, which is the ring-like collar around the midsection of the body. These secretions harden into a tube, which then forms into a cocoon that may contain up to 20 minuscule worm embryos. Typically, only two or three offspring from each cocoon survive. The cocoons may hatch within weeks in warm weather, but cocoons that are created in the winter may remain dormant until springtime.

Worms digest compost material by grinding it as it passes through their bodies. Their castings, which are rich in nutrients, are essentially a mild fertilizer, not compost, and you can spread them directly onto garden soil or in flowerpots, container gardens, and window boxes. Castings can also be diluted in a mixture of ten parts water to one part castings and used as liquid fertilizer for use on the ground, or as a foliar fertilizer, which is one that is sprayed directly onto the leaves.

USE CAUTION WITH NON-NATIVE WORM SPECIES

If you order worms online or through a store or garden center, make sure that they are native to your area. The vendor should be able to tell you what areas of the country the worms are native to. If you are using a non-native worm species, make sure they do not escape into the wild. As with any other invasive species, non-native worms can wreak havoc on the local ecosystem. Some, such as red wigglers, reproduce very rapidly. In 11 weeks, one red wiggler worm can produce up to 99 offspring. They can disrupt the environment in hardwood forests by eating the leaf litter too quickly. The leaf litter on the forest floor provides cover for hard-shelled nuts, and without it, the nuts cannot mature into trees. Removing the leaf litter prematurely also affects the pH balance of the soil and can cause erosion. The introduction of worms into northern climates where they did not formerly exist has caused changes in the kind of plants that grow there.

Worm species

There are several species of worms acceptable for use in worm composting.

- European Night Crawlers, also called dew worms, are very large worms. While they do not reproduce quickly, making only about 38 cocoons per year, they can eat coarse materials, such as paper and cardboard. They are often present in outdoor compost piles. They typically reach lengths of 5 to 10 inches and can live for three to six years. They are dark red, and their head end turns grayish as they age. They get their name from their habit of crawling on the surface of the ground at night while they search for food. They pull organic materials down into tunnels that can be as much as 6 feet deep. This helps nourish soil from below and allows air and water to filter down into the soil. Night crawlers are best left outdoors because their habits are not conducive to indoor vermicomposting.

- Red worms, or red wigglers, are the most common type of worm sold for composting. They are mostly red with a pale yellow bottom and range in size from 1 to 4 inches long when fully grown. They can live for two to three years and prefer to stay near the surface, often under compost or manure. They also congregate under objects on the ground when the soil is saturated with water. They produce 70 to 100 cocoons per year.

• Tiger worms can be identified by a characteristic red and yellow stripe pattern. They are similar in habit to manure worms and compost worms, which are purple, red, or maroon. All three species grow to be between 1 and 5 inches and can live up to four years. They reproduce quickly, making up to 400 cocoons per year. These worms do not burrow into the soil, preferring to live under manure and compost heaps. Because of this tendency, and their very fast reproduction cycle, they make great vermicompost worms.

HOW MANY WORMS DO I NEED?

Red Wiggler worms can double their population in one to three months in a well-maintained worm bin. Mature worms can eat up to half their own body weight in scraps daily.

To determine how many worms you need, weigh your food scraps every day for a week. If your household produces 1 pound of scraps per day, you will need 2 pounds of worms, or approximately 2,000 worms. The worm bin should be large enough to allow 1 square foot of surface area per pound of scraps. If you produce 2 pounds of scraps per day, you will need a bin with a surface area of at least 2 square feet. Worms will quickly reproduce, and within a year, you can end up with 15,000 to 20,000 worms in your worm bin.

If your worm bin becomes over crowded, you can separate some of the worms and put them in a new bin. If you do not need a second bin at home, consider sharing your worms (and your knowledge) with a friend, or keeping a bin at work to eat scraps from lunches. You might also consider donating a new bin complete with worms, fresh bedding, and instructions to a school where the children can learn about composting.

Buying your worms

If you are making the bin yourself, you should purchase the worms through a garden-supply company that will provide the right kind of worms. You can buy worms from WormsWrangler **(http:// wormswrangler.com)** or Wormfarm.com **(www.wormfarm.com)**. Ordinary earthworms that you can dig up in your yard are not the best candidates for a worm bin because they are not used to eating a rich diet and can only live in soil, not compost. Vermicomposting incorporates special species of worms that have been bred to live on a diet of household waste. The most common type of composting worms, red wigglers, sells for between $20 and $45 per pound depending on the source.

Worm Bins

You can either purchase or make a worm bin. If you are just start-ing out, it is easier to buy a system that already has everything you need, including the right number and species of worms.

Buying a worm bin

You can purchase worm bins from many garden supply stores and from several websites. When buying a bin, think of the cost, the quality of the bin itself, how it will look in your home or yard, and how easy it is to maintain the bin and collect the castings. Worm bins come in a wide variety of styles and range in price from about $43 for a small wooden bin to up to more than $600 for large, insulated, heated bins.

Vermicompost bins all include a way to collect the liquid that drains out of the compost and a way to drain it off without disturbing the worms. Some commercial bins have several trays that are stacked in layers, one on top of the other. You put the worms in their bedding on the bottom layer, and as that layer fills with castings, you add fresh bedding and food to the upper layers so that the worms can eat their way to the top. The bottoms of the trays are usually made of some kind of porous material, such as plastic screening, with openings big enough for the worms to climb through. The bottom usually has a drip pan to catch the liquid that drains out of the compost. On most types of stackable worm bins, you can remove the castings from the lower layers of the stack without disturbing the worms by simply pulling out the tray.

Making your own worm bin

To begin a worm bin, first figure out where you are going to put it. Worms like to be cool, preferring temperatures between 50 and 84 degrees, so an indoor spot in a basement or mudroom is ideal. You can also keep the bin in an enclosed porch or unheated closet as long as the temperature does not get too hot or cold. It should be some place where you will remember to feed them and not in an area, such as a garage, where they might freeze or die of heat. If you can afford a heated, insulated worm bin, then you can place it in a cooler area as long as you have a reliable source of power to run the thermostat and heater. You can put your worms outdoors on nice days as long as they are protected from the sun and predators. The bin should always have a ventilated lid to keep the worms contained, whether it is kept indoors or out. If you have small children, you may want to use a bungee cord or ratchet strap to hold the lid on and keep kids from playing in the compost.

To start the worm bin, gather the materials and order the worms ahead of time. You will have to keep the worms chilled until their new home is ready. Keeping them very cool will slow their metabolism so that they do not starve before they are placed in their new home. They can be kept in a refrigerator for a day or two. The cold will make them sluggish, but should not kill them. Make sure to keep them moist because worms breathe through their skin. If your worms dry out, they can die within minutes. Also, make sure that they are not in an airtight bag or container. The container they were shipped in should provide a good environment to keep them in. Always check with the store or website you buy the worms from to get their recommendations for storing them until you are ready to put them into the bin.

You can make your own worm bin from a variety of materials. These instructions describe how to make one using a plastic tub or trash can. You may want to use rubber instead of plastic because plastic will eventually split and crack and rubber will last longer. Galvanized tubs can also work, as can wooden boxes. Make sure that your container is no deeper than 2 feet because composting worms will not burrow any deeper than that. The total size of the container will depend on how many scraps your family produces.

Supplies and Tools

- A large tub, trash can, or box (If you are using a rubber or plastic bin, make sure it is opaque so that no light can get in to disturb the worms.)

- A lid for the container to keep the light out and worms in

- A piece of plastic window screen large enough to cover the bottom and up the insides of the bin (This will keep the worms from crawling out through the air holes.)

- Drill, 1-inch drill bit, ⅛-inch drill bit

- ½-inch cork (optional)

- ½-inch drill bit (optional)

- Plastic pan larger than the tub or trash can and deep enough to hold a couple of inches of water

- Bricks or a wooden frame to keep the bin off the floor

- Bedding for the bin (see below)

Instructions

1. Drill 1-inch holes every few inches around the top of the plastic container to allow air in.

2. Drill several ⅛-inch holes in the sides of the container, starting approximately 4 inches from the bottom. These holes will provide ventilation in plastic, rubber, or metal tubs. They are not necessary in wooden boxes as long as there are cracks and openings between the boards.

3. Drill ⅛-inch holes in the bottom of the container.

4. Use a watertight container under the bin to catch the liquid. Place a few bricks or boards in the watertight container; then place the bin on top of these bricks to keep it up out of the water. It is best if this container is on a raised surface like a countertop or table and has a tap on

it so you can easily drain the liquid without disturbing the worms.

5. You can create a makeshift tap by drilling a ½-inch hole on one corner of the container and plugging it with a ½-inch cork. Remove the cork when you want to drain off the water. If you keep your bin outdoors, you can just let the liquid seep out onto the ground, or let it evaporate if you do not plan to use it.

6. Place the plastic window screen inside the bin, making sure all the air holes are covered with the screen.

Filling the worm bin

1. Place a 3- to 4-inch layer of bedding on the bottom of the bin. The bedding can be leaf mold, sifted compost, shredded newspaper or cardboard, rotten sawdust or wood chips, or a mixture of these items. If using paper or cardboard, soak it in water for about ten minutes and shred it into pieces smaller than 3 inches by 3 inches. Cardboard has a relatively high pH value, but worms will still eat it and use it for shelter. If using wood chips, soak them in water overnight to dampen them, and squeeze out the excess water before putting it into the bin. The bedding must be kept damp because the worms will suffocate if they dry out.

2. Place the worms on top of the damp bedding and cover them with 1 or 2 inches of dry shredded newspaper. Let the worms get used to this new environment for a few days.

3. When you notice that they have started to eat the bedding, it is time to feed them. Feed them only half the normal amount for the first two to four weeks until they get com-

fortable. The "normal amount" will depend on how many worms you have and how many scraps your household produces. In the initial stages, feed them only about a ½ pound per day until they get used to their new home.

4. Slowly increase the amount you feed them over the course of a few weeks, up to the maximum amount for your bin, so as not to overwhelm them.

5. Keep in mind that you will have to provide fresh bedding about once a month or as needed. You may need to increase the amount of bedding you provide as the population of worms increases.

A worm bin fed entirely on kitchen scraps mixed with paper or cardboard will give you compost that is high in humic acid that is very beneficial to plants. Humic acid is a natural by-product of the microbes that decay plant material. It is found in all non-sterile soil, but compost contains a much higher amount of it because of how compost is made. Humic acid is not a fertilizer, but acts as a complement to fertilizer. According to Natural Environmental Systems (**www.naturalenviro.com**), humic acid:

• Adds organic matter to organically deficient soils

• Increases root vitality

• Improves nutrient uptake

• Increases chlorophyll synthesis

• Allows for better seed germination

• Increases fertilizer retention

• Stimulates beneficial microbial activity

- Results in healthier plants and improved yields

Now that you have filled your worm bin and your worms are getting settled in, what should you feed them?

What to Feed (and Not Feed) Your Worms

When you purchase your worms, the dealer should let you know what foods they can consume most easily and what foods you should avoid feeding them. Worms can eat many things that cannot be put into an outdoor compost pile, including bread and cooked food scraps. Worms can safely eat fresh or cooked vegetables, most fruit (although not the pits), leaves, paper, tea leaves, and coffee grounds.

In general, you want to avoid large quantities of raw fruit and vegetable matter. This should go into the outdoor compost bin instead. If you do not have an outdoor bin, you can give these foods to the worms, but citrus peels should be avoided because they contain limonene, which can be poisonous to worms. A surplus of citrus or coffee grounds can also change the pH of the bin by making it acidic and killing the worms. If you notice that your worms are not eating a particular kind of food, just take it out of the bin and feed them something else. They often avoid odorous foods such as garlic, onions, and broccoli, but let them try these anyway. Your worms might like them, and that will be one less thing you have to throw away.

You should avoid feeding worms any kind of food with seeds (such as peppers, squash, tomatoes, cucumbers) because worms will not eat the seeds, and there will not be enough heat generated in a worm bin to kill the seeds. This means the fruits or vegetables may start growing in your worm bin or later in your garden. If you completely remove the seeds from peppers, then you can feed worms the flesh of sweet peppers. Do not feed them hot peppers because the same substance (capsaicin) that burns your mouth will hurt the worms.

Worms typically avoid eating parts of plants that have the potential to grow, such as potato peels with eyes and the tops of root vegetables like carrots and turnips. You may want to avoid feeding your worms these types of foods, or puree them before feeding them.

Worms like stale or moldy bread and leftover pasta (just do not give them pasta with an oily sauce, such as fettuccine Alfredo, because the oil is not good for the bin.) Plain corn meal will give worms a lot of energy in a hurry, but be sure there are no other ingredients in it. Worms need a source of grit in their diet to help them digest fibrous plant matter. One good source of grit is very finely ground eggshells. Rinse the whites from cracked shells, grind the shells in a food processor, mortar and pestle, or with a rolling pin and sprinkle the calcium-rich grit into the worm bin. You can also sprinkle some sand into the bin.

As with an outdoor compost bin, adding greens will increase the nitrogen content, and adding browns will increase the carbon and phosphate. If your worm bin gets too hot, too wet, or smelly, you should increase the amount of brown materials, the same way you would with a regular compost bin in that condition. Worms need greens (kitchen scraps) to eat, so you will need to continue feeding them the required amount according to how many worms you have. You may also add composted cow manure or uncomposted rabbit, sheep, or goat manure to the worm bin. Bury the manure at least 3 inches down in the bin.

You should not feed worms vinegar, hot peppers, sauces, oils, greasy foods, fresh grass clippings, dairy products, fruit pits, or very salty or very sweet foods because each of these foods can cause problems in the bin. Vinegar will change the acidity of the bin, making it inhospitable to the worms. Hot peppers can burn the worms the same way they burn your skin. Sauces, oils, and greasy foods can suffocate the worms. Fresh grass clippings will decompose very quickly and will heat up the bin, which can kill the worms. They may also make an anaerobic mess just as they can in outdoor bins. Dairy products will spoil and smell bad. Fruit pits are too big for worms to eat and will not decompose. They may also take root and begin growing. Salt or salty foods will kill the worms by dehydrating them, and sweet, sugary foods can cause an overgrowth of yeast in the bin, which can be as harmful to the worms as a yeast infection is to humans.

You should not feed meat to your worms. Rotting meat stinks and will attract flies, which lay their eggs on it. While small amounts of cooked meat can be buried in outdoor vermicomposting bins and regular compost heaps, there is always a chance that you will invite unwanted creatures into your yard. If you live in an area where raccoons, rats, foxes, possum, or other carnivores visit your yard, you should probably avoid composting meat altogether. Even neighborhood dogs can be a nuisance if they find meat in your compost.

In an indoor bin, the smell of rotting meat alone will convince you not to use it. Generally, composting meat is something that only experienced composters take on, and then only if they have a very fast-decomposing hot heap to put it in. You can give it a try, but if the worms are not eating it quickly, or if odor becomes a problem, stop feeding meat and fish and stick to non-animal scraps.

To prepare kitchen scraps for your worms, run them through a blender or food processor, perhaps with some water. The smaller the pieces are, the easier it will be for the worms to eat. Because they do not have teeth, they can take in only very small particles of food. Feed the worms about three times a week once the bin is established. At first, you may want to feed them weekly, especially as they are becoming acclimated to their new home. Feed them by spreading small amounts of kitchen waste just under the bedding. Spreading shredded newspaper over the food will discourage fruit flies and other pests and encourage the worms to come to the top of the bin to eat. Do not pile the newspaper on thick or the waste will start to compost and the bin will heat up, killing the worms. Feeding your worms a small amount of food every day or two will help them reproduce, which is what you want when starting a new bin. Feeding them a large quantity of food less frequently (once a week or so) will lead to fatter worms, so if you plan to use your worms for fish bait, this will be a good thing.

Make sure to feed them only as much as they can eat and not more, because you do not want the food to rot or start to compost. As a guideline, worms can eat half their own weight in food each day, so if you start off with 2 pounds of worms, feed them 1 pound of food in small meals over the course of the day. As the worms reproduce, you will have to increase the amount you are feeding them. Increase the amount of food slowly over the course of several weeks. If there is not enough food, the worms will be able to eat their bedding for a few days until you get the balance just right. Because it is not possible to know exactly how many worms you have once they start reproducing, you will have to keep an eye on how much food they eat. If there are a lot of leftovers and the food is spoiling, give them less. If all the food is eaten up quickly, give them a bit more.

Place the food under shredded newspapers on top of the bedding, but not in the castings. The castings are a waste product and worms do not like to live in them. The castings will generally be toward the bottom of the bin because worms tend to eat in an upward direction. However, they will be obvious when you see them because they resemble shiny dark coffee grounds. You will need to add more shredded newspaper as the worms consume the older bedding. This will help to keep the contents of the bin from getting soggy. Worms prefer to live under the shelter it will provide.

Do not worry if you have to go away on vacation for a week or two because your worms can live by eating their bedding. Simply feed them before you go away, and make sure there is enough fresh bedding so that they can eat the paper if they run out of food scraps.

HOW MUCH SHOULD I FEED MY WORMS?

If you are concerned about how much to feed your worms, there is a simple method called the quadrant system. Used in the vermicomposting curricula provided free to school teachers, this system is easy enough for children to understand. Begin by imagining that the worm bin is divided into four quadrants. If you are doing this with children, it might help to draw lines on the outside of the bin, and number them as below. This will also help in case your bin is turned around and you are no longer sure which corner is which.

1	2
4	3

Begin burying food in quadrant number one. A few days later, place food in quadrant number two. A few days after that, place food in quadrant three, and so on, until you are back to quadrant one. If there is still food in quadrant number one when you go to feed, that is a signal that you are overfeeding the worms. Give them some time to eat what is already in the bin, and then begin again. This time, feed them less often and give them a smaller amount of food. However, if you get to quadrant one and the worms have already eaten up all the food in quadrants one, two, and three, you may want to give them a little more food or feed them more often.

Harvesting the castings

It may take six or seven months before your worm bin produces enough castings to use in your garden. Once a new bin becomes established, the worms will eat more because they will have started to reproduce and, thus, will have more castings. After the first harvest of castings, you should be able to gather it about every three months.

Worms generally start eating at the bottom of the bin and work their way to the top, leaving their castings behind on the lower layers as they move up. There are several ways to remove the castings, but, essentially, you will have to move the worms and the top layer of compost aside or into another container to get to the castings. The contents of the bin may be sticky and mud like, so you may want to wear gloves.

It may be easier to harvest if you tip the bin on its side with a layer of newspapers under it to catch anything that falls out or if you dump the contents of the bin a little at a time into a large shallow pan or tray. Do this outside on a warm sunny day or point a bright light at the compost because the light will cause the worms to burrow into the bedding. This process can take ten to 15 minutes. Remove the castings from the top of the pile by hand, being careful not to capture any worms along with it. Doing this by hand allows you to sort through the castings and return any stray worms to the bin (or put them into a newly prepared bin, if you are separating the worms). After you have removed the castings down to the level where the worms have burrowed, you may need to wait and let them burrow deeper before harvesting the next layer.

You can watch a video of Bentley Christie, the Compost Guy, retrieving worms from a bin at **www.youtube.com/watch?v=h6h3N8OIQYM**. This video shows Christie using a bright light method to cause his worms to burrow and then sifting out the castings by hand. You can find out more about vermicomposting on his website: **www.redwormcomposting.com/**.

After you have removed the castings, put in fresh bedding, replace the worms and the compost material on top of the bedding, and let the worms keep working. Some commercial stacking worm bins make this step easy and allow you to remove the bottom layer of the stack, dump out the castings, and replace the empty container on the top.

You can also sort out vermicompost by pushing the contents of the bin to one side and filling the other side with fresh bedding and food. After a couple of weeks, the worms will have migrated over to where the food is and you can scoop out the castings from the vacated side of the bin. Some people even use a sheet of cardboard pushed vertically most of the way into the bin to divide it. The worms can burrow under the cardboard to the side with the food, and the cardboard helps you know where to start scooping. This is a slow process, but it helps ensure that you are not scooping out worms along with the castings.

After you have retrieved the castings and sorted the worms out, you will need to dry the castings before you can store them. You can dry castings by spreading them on layers of newspaper to dry in the sun. Check the castings carefully for stray worms, because they will die if left to dry out. Once the castings are dry, sift them through a plastic colander with large holes. Return any undigested food bits to the bin. Castings can be stored in plastic buckets or containers as long as you drill or punch holes in the sides to allow air to circulate. Keep castings very lightly damp by occasionally spritzing them with water from a spray bottle, and give them proper ventilation to help maintain the biologically active components.

How to Make Worm Tea

Worm tea is similar to compost tea, but has a few extra ingredients. Molasses or corn syrup provides food for the microorganisms. Rainwater is the best type of water to use, but you can use water straight from the tap if you have a well. If you have a municipal water supply that is treated with chlorine, leave the bucket of water sitting out overnight to allow the chemicals to dissipate. If you have a rainwater cistern, you can use this as well. If your cistern is filled by chemically treated water that has been trucked in, then the same caveat applies as for municipal water — let it sit out overnight to let volatile chemicals dissipate.

Do not worry if you cannot collect two cups of castings from your worm bin on the first try. Just follow the instructions above for drying and storing castings, and save them up until you have enough to make worm tea.

Supplies and Tools

- 2 cups worm castings

- 2 tablespoons corn syrup or molasses

- 5-gallon bucket

- Old sock or pantyhose (with no holes)

- Water

Instructions

1. Pour the castings into the sock or stocking, and tie it closed.

2. Submerge the stocking in the water.

3. Add the corn syrup or molasses to the water.

4. Let the castings soak for at least 24 hours, stirring often.

5. Use within 48 hours to water potted plants, flower beds, or gardens.

Optionally, you may use an aquarium bubbler to aerate the mixture. Follow the instructions and precautions on the package when setting up the bubbler.

Using worm tea

As with regular compost tea, worm tea can be added to your gardens and houseplants. It can also be used as a foliar fertilizer and sprayed on plants. If you have enough vermicompost, you can brew up very large batches of worm tea so you have enough for a vegetable garden. If you are very dedicated to vermicomposting, you may have enough to sell to friends and neighbors.

Troubleshooting a Worm Bin

Like any compost system, worm bins can have problems if they are not properly maintained. Most of these problems are easy to resolve and avoid if you take some precautions. Below are some symptoms of problems that might arise in vermicomposting bins and what to do about them.

Symptoms	Cause	Solution
Unconsumed or moldy food	Overfeeding	You have to feed worms only as much as they can eat so that the food does not rot or start to compost. The worms may ignore certain foods, such as onions, broccoli, garlic, onions, citrus, and other strong-smelling foods. If this happens, stop feeding that particular kind of food because it will rot. If food starts to go moldy, and the worms do not eat it, remove it from the bin to prevent the spread of molds in the bedding. While mold will not kill the worms, it can indicate that the bin is too acidic; if not remedied, this will eventually cause problems. Make sure to air out a bin that has had mold in it, and keep a close eye on it to make sure the balance goes back to normal.
Worms are sluggish, not eating much	Lack of air	Worms need to breathe and need a supply of fresh air. If the bin does not have enough ventilation holes, or if the holes have become plugged, the worms can become sluggish. Check that the air holes are clear, and leave the lid off the bin for a few hours to let air in.

Symptoms	Cause	Solution
Worms trying to escape	Too much moisture (see also, "Too much light")	If your bin develops mold or your worms try to escape, you may have a problem with moisture. Just like after a heavy rain when worms burrow to the top of the soil, worms in a wet bin will wriggle up to the top in an effort not to drown. They may climb right out of the bin if they have to. You have to empty the liquid from the bottom of the bin regularly to keep the worms from drowning. If the bin has holes in the bottom and is set up on bricks so the liquid has somewhere to drain, you do not have to worry about your worms drowning. If your bin does not have drainage holes, you can suck the liquid up with a turkey baster. If there is any mold in the bin, wipe it out with paper towels, and then tear the towel up for the worms to eat. While most molds are harmless to the worms, black or green molds may give off spores that can be harmful to humans. If you have any sort of breathing difficulty or allergies, be very careful if you see black or green mold in your bin. You may want to air the bin out by leaving it outdoors in a shaded spot until the mold subsides. If you are worried, you can always move the worms to a new bin, and thoroughly clean the old one. If you use limestone to dry out a worm bin, make sure to add only a very small amount and to stir it in well over several days, because it can react with the compost and release carbon dioxide, which will suffocate the worms.
Bedding dried out, worms dying, or not reproducing	Too little moisture	If the bin dries out completely, the worms can suffocate from the lack of moisture. If the bin is damp, but not damp enough, the worms may stop reproducing. When you feed the worms, turn the compost over with your hand (you may wish to wear gloves for this), and check to make sure that all the paper in the bin is damp. If not, spray it with water from a spray bottle until it is moistened.

Symptoms	Cause	Solution
Bin smells bad or worms dying	Too much heat	Just like with a normal compost bin, if you add too many nitrogen-rich, green items, the compost will heat up. This heat can kill the worms, so make sure to add a very small amount of green products in comparison to brown. You must keep the bin at a reasonable temperature so that the worms do not dry out and die. Insulated bins help keep the worms warm enough in cool climates and seasons. Bins with thermostats are expensive, but do help regulate the temperature.
Worms trying to escape	Too much light (see also, "Too much moisture")	The bin must be opaque because worms do not like bright light. Keeping the bin in a lighted area will discourage worms from climbing out of the bin, but too much light can make them unhappy and keep them from eating and reproducing the way they should.
Insect pests invading the bin	Bin is too wet or food is not buried in bedding	Mites can infest a bin that stays too wet. These will look like very tiny red or brown dots. Most mites are not harmful to the worms, although there are one or two species that are parasitic to insects. According to Bentley Christie of Redwormcomposting.com, these parasitic mites typically attack arthropods (creatures like beetles and spiders) and do not attack worms. You can read more about worm bin mites on his blog: **www.redwormcomposting.com/worm-bin-creatures/parasitic-worm-bin-mites/**. If you want to get rid of mites, drain the liquid or add more shredded newspaper to dry the bin a little bit. To test to see if you got all the mites, put a slice of bread on top of the food and leave it overnight. If there are mites on it in the morning, cut back on feedings or add more bedding to dry the bin further. The presence of mites will not harm the finished product — the castings, but they can be unnerving and unsightly.

Symptoms	Cause	Solution
		Fruit flies are another common pest and will typically be attracted by fruit waste in the bin. To discourage them, bury the food scraps under the bedding. You can also lure them away by placing a cup of cider vinegar near the bin. The flies will be attracted to the vinegar and drown in it. Do not place the cup in the bin because the acidic vinegar will be toxic to the worms. Pot worms are tiny pink or white worms that live in healthy soil. They eat fungi and like to live in very damp environments where fungi are plentiful. If you see several of these little worms (they are less than $1/2$ inch long), it could mean that your bin is too damp. On the bright side, these worms make excellent castings and will not tolerate soils contaminated with heavy metals such as lead or copper, so their presences means your bin is healthy (albeit too damp). Ants may infest your bin if they find it on food-foraging journeys. If they do, use store-bought ant traps outside the bin. Make sure the bin is moist enough because ants prefer to live in dry areas and will not come into your bin if it is damp. Pour a line of borax around the ant bin because ants (and other insects) will die if they crawl across borax, but it is harmless to humans. Ants will eat worms, and the scouts that locate a food source (in this case your worm bin) will lead all their fellow ants to the bin to harvest the food and take it back to their nest, and so they must be dealt with immediately. Centipedes are carnivorous insects and will eat worms if they can. They like to live in moist areas, so make sure the worm bin is not too damp. If you can catch them, you can release them outside or kill them. You may be able to place sticky insect traps around the bin to prevent centipedes from crawling into the bin in the first place.

Symptoms	Cause	Solution
Animal pests invading the bin	Bin not in a secure location or not properly covered	Keep the bin away from animals that might try to break into it to eat the scraps and the worms. If you place the bin outside, make sure that it is securely covered to keep birds, raccoons, possums, and other small animals from digging in it. Birds will want to eat the worms and larger animals may go after the food at first, but quickly discover the worms and wipe out your bin in an afternoon.

RUNAWAY WORMS!

Worms may be confused or agitated when they are first transported to their new home because they are very sensitive to vibrations. This keeps them alive when they are in the ground because they can detect the vibrations caused by a predator's footsteps. However, in a worm bin this can cause trouble. To keep worms from escaping, leave the bin uncovered in a well-lit room for a few days (or shine a lamp on the bin). This should keep the worms burrowed safely into the center of the bin until they calm down. Do this any time you move the bin to a new location, such as when you move it indoors after having it outside in the summer.

Worms may also flee the bin if it is too hot, too wet, or overcrowded. Make sure to drain water from the bin, keep enough bedding in it to absorb excess water, and keep it in a relatively cool place. If overcrowding is a problem, start a new bin, release some of the worms into your outdoor compost pile or garden, or share them with friends. Keep in mind that compost worms such as red wigglers are bred for and are used to a very food-rich environment, so if you do want to set them free, the compost pile will be the most comfortable place for them.

Where to Use Vermicompost

Like regular compost, vermicompost can be used everywhere in the garden or wherever you have plantings. Unlike regular compost, vermicompost contains more than just nutrients. A worm's intestinal tract produces enzymes that have antibiotic, insecticidal, and fungicidal properties. These chemicals not only protect the worm, but these enzymes also help plants resist disease and insect infestation when worm castings are used to amend the soil around them. For this reason, worm castings, whether from wild worms or in the concentrated form of vermicompost, are vital to the health of all your house and garden plants.

Here are some ways to include vermicompost in your garden:

- Use vermicompost in flowerpots and containers. Mix about 20 percent vermicompost to 80 percent potting soil. The vermicompost will give a gentle fertilization to the flowers and the potting soil gives the roots something to cling to.

- Use vermicompost as a top dressing in tired out flowerpots and containers. Spread about ¼ inch of vermicompost on the surface before watering. The vermicompost will release nutrients slowly into the soil and feed the plants rather than shocking them as a large dose of synthetic fertilizer might.

- Use vermicompost on outdoor flower beds by spreading it on the soil beneath the mulch and watering thoroughly.

- Mix vermicompost into planting holes for shrubs, trees, and perennials. The slow release of nitrogen will encourage rooting while not burning tender roots.

For a complete lesson in vermicomposting, read *Worms Eat Our Garbage* by the late Mary Appelhof. Known as "The Worm Lady," Appelhof is well-known in compost circles for her efforts to tell the world about worm composting. Her website, **www.wormwoman.com**, contains several back issues of her newsletter, WormWoman's *WormEzine* and a wealth of information on vermicomposting, including how to winterize a worm bin, how to harvest worm castings, and making and using worm casting tea.

CASE STUDY

Kimberly Roy
Amateur composter
Middletown, New Jersey

I love taking part in creating rich, organic matter to use for plants. I began composting about ten years ago while living on the north shore of Lake Tahoe, California. I loved plants, but there was no soil there because the terrain consisted of rock, sand, and evergreens. Potting soil was not only an extra expense, but also difficult to obtain because my main mode of transportation was a bike or the bus. After doing some research at the local library on vermicomposting, I began raising worms and making my own dirt and plant food with compost tea.

I ordered a 2-pound bag of about 500 Canadian earthworms. These guys were 6 inches long and about the diameter of a pencil. I settled them into their new home — a plastic foam cooler with shredded and moistened bedding and food scraps, set this cooler in the kitchen of my small studio apartment, and went out for the evening. Upon coming home, I was horrified to find worms all over the place. They covered the white linoleum kitchen floor, the carpet of the main living space, and a few had even made it into the bathroom.

It is important not to over feed worms as the waste turns anaerobic and toxic. If compost stinks badly, the worms will want to leave. It becomes a very unhealthy place for them.

Occasionally, I put some pieces of vegetable scrapings, eggshells, tea bags, or other non-meat or dairy food scraps into the worm bin for food. The worms eat and digest the organic matter at a faster pace than it would decompose on its own. The worms simply could not eat all the scraps we produce, and the food would turn rotten, smelly, and toxic for the worms, so we put some of it on the outside pile. We shovel or rake this highly nutritious material into selected areas of the garden or use it to supplement potting soil.

If done right, composting is a rewarding and enjoyable hobby. I enjoy the smell of dirt and raising worms. It is neat when they have babies.

CHAPTER 9

WINTER AND INDOOR COMPOSTING

Composting continues even in the winter, although it happens at a reduced rate. Bacteria can survive at very low temperatures, and they keep digesting matter even when the compost pile is covered in snow. To help the bacteria work a little longer in the fall and start working earlier in the spring, it is a good idea to insulate outdoor compost bins with carpeting or old blankets and tarps. Simply cover the bin, and if it has open sides, surround it with your chosen insulator. You can also surround and cover outdoor compost piles with bales of straw or hay. The more heat the pile can retain, the longer and more vigorously it will work throughout the winter. Cover the bin when the outdoor temperatures cool down, or whenever it is convenient for you.

Winter Worm Bins?

It is possible to winterize worm bins, and some composters have even had success with worm windrows. A **windrow** is any row of vegetation that has been heaped up as if by the wind, but a person can also create a windrow on purpose. One such person is Bentley Christie, owner of the website Red Worm Composting (**www.redwormcomposting.com**).

Starting in late fall 2009, Christie built a large worm windrow in his backyard in Ontario, Canada. He used rotted pumpkin waste, grass clippings, horse manure, a large amount of leaves, and rotted straw. He then covered the whole thing with a large tarp to keep the heat in. A short while later, he pushed aside the top layer of leaves and straw and added most of the contents of an outdoor worm bin, including the worms. At this point (early December), the protected windrow had an internal temperature of about 68 degrees. After a snowfall, the temperature in the windrow went down, so he added more rotted straw (with worms) and a large amount of coffee grounds.

About a month later, the pile had cooled to a disappointing 39 degrees, and the top layer had frozen. Armed with food scraps and coffee grounds that had been warmed to room temperature by bringing them for several days, Christie pulled the windrow apart and inserted a string of rope lights that are commonly used to decorate decks. He then added shredded cardboard, hay, coffee grounds, more hay, and then the warmed food scraps. He watered the bin, added some Bokashi microbes, and then covered the whole thing with a blanket before replacing the tarp. The later addition of a little molasses and some water, as well as a hot water bottle, warmed the windrow up, and a couple of days later the temperature was back above 60 degrees.

By the end of January, the windrow had mostly started to warm up again, and Christie added some horse manure, fresh straw, more water, and more molasses. Additions of food waste, leaves, and grass helped increase the temperature even more, and by the end of February, the temperature was between 77 and 86 degrees. He found red worms and springtails in the pile and fed it again with alfalfa and molasses water. **Springtails** are tiny insects, usually only 1 to 2 millimeters long, but sometimes up to 6 millimeters, or about a ¼ inch, that spring or jump when disturbed. They eat plants, pollen, and other small particles and are usually beneficial to a worm bin.

To read about all the ups and downs of Christie's winter composting with worms, check out the links at the bottom of this blog post: **www.redwormcomposting.com/winter-composting/winter-worm-windrow%E2%80%9302-22-10/**. As you can see, winter composting is possible; it just takes a lot of work and a large amount of ingredients.

A warm, healthy bin will steam as the weather cools in the fall, but there is little chance of overheating your compost. Temperatures up to 150 degrees are desirable in your compost, and it is unlikely the bin will get hotter than that in the late fall and winter in most parts of the United States. If you are concerned about overheating the pile, check the temperature of your pile on a warm day and if necessary, uncover it, and turn or stir it to let it cool down. If using a plastic tarp, remember to remove it when the weather begins to warm up in the spring so that you do not overheat the pile or cause moisture build up. Monitoring the pile with a remote sensor thermometer or taking frequent readings with a probe thermometer are good ways to stay aware of the state of your compost. This will allow you to make additions to it throughout the winter, assuming you can get to it through the snow, and will let you know when it is "waking up" in the spring.

Indoor Composting

Indoor composting is ideal all year round if you live in an apartment or condominium with a small yard, or if you do not generate enough waste to feed a large compost pile. It is also good for people who only need a small amount of compost to use in window boxes or container gardens, and it is a good alternative for people who normally keep an outdoor bin, but cannot access it in the winter. Indoor composting means that all the food scraps from winter holiday feasts will be composted instead of sent to the landfill, and you can keep generating compost even when the weather is bad. There are several products on the market for indoor composting, including small countertop or under counter systems and larger indoor bins. Even vermicomposting can be done indoors if you have a room where you can control the temperature.

Pros and cons of indoor composting

To determine if indoor composting is right for you, check out this list of pros and cons.

Pros

- You do not need a yard or garden.

- You do not have to do a lot of physical labor.

- You do not need a lot of space.

- Some indoor composting systems can consume meat, small bones, and other waste that you generally cannot put into an outdoor system.

- It may be less expensive than maintaining an outdoor system.

- You do not have to worry about attracting animals to your property.

- You do not have to worry about the concerns of neighbors.

Cons

- Depending on the system you choose, it may be more expensive than maintaining a low-tech outdoor system.

- Indoor composting takes up some space.

- It may cause foul odors if not properly maintained.

- It may attract flies if not properly maintained.

- If you do not have a yard, container gardens, or houseplants, you will have to find a way to dispose of the compost.

If the pros outweigh the cons for you, then go ahead and start indoor composting. Following are some ways you can begin composting inside.

Indoor trash bag composting

The easiest way to compost indoors is in a simple trash bag. This will produce an anaerobic compost mixture that smells quite bad when first opened. Remember that aerobic composting uses a lot of oxygen and, therefore, does not have the same rank smell as anaerobic composting. After the compost is fully decomposed, you will have to rake it out onto the soil to dry to eliminate most of the smell. After it has dried for three or four days, you will be able to use the compost as normal.

Supplies and Tools

- Sturdy 32-gallon trash bag

Instructions

1. Keep the bag inside in a warm place, such as a heated garage. If it gets cold or freezes, it will not produce compost. You definitely do not want to keep this inside your house because of the noxious smell produced by anaerobic decomposition. If you do not have a garage to keep it in, do this kind of composting only in warm weather.

2. Fill the bag with a combination of leaves, food scraps, grass clippings, finished compost, if you have it, and an activator such as alfalfa meal.

3. Close the bag and shake it daily to mix the contents. Water it if the contents dry out. Add dry grass clippings and leaves if the contents are too wet.

4. When the bag is full, hold your breath, and dump it on the ground. Rake the compost out on the ground and expose it to the air for three to four days to dry out before using it as you would any other compost.

If your compost is ready before spring, leave it bagged up. You definitely do not want to try to dry it out indoors. This is a good project for an early spring day when there is a nice breeze blowing. The breeze will help dry the compost quickly and will blow the smell away.

Commercial Indoor Compost Bins

There are a wide variety of indoor compost systems. These range in size from very small home systems to large commercial systems used in restaurants and other environments that generate a lot of waste. Choosing the system that is right for you depends on the space you have available, the cost of the system, and how much composting you would like to do. This section discusses several commercially available systems that can be used inside. *Sources for these systems are listed in the Appendix.*

Non-electric indoor systems

Non-electric systems use a variety of methods to decompose the scraps put into them. Some use fermentation, usually with the assistance of added microorganisms. These systems convert the carbohydrates in the scraps into alcohols, carbon dioxide, or organic acids. For comparison, think of the way yeast ferments when you are baking bread. It consumes the flour and creates carbon dioxide bubbles in the dough. If you let bread dough rise for too long, it will take on an unpleasant sour taste and smell from the alcohols the fermentation process releases. Fermenting compost systems will also have that sour smell because they are anaerobic systems. Most of these systems will be air-tight and enclosed, so there will only be a smell if you open it during the fermentation process.

Non-electric systems also include worm bins used in vermicomposting, which is a non-electric (although not anaerobic) process.

Effective Microorganism Bokashi Compost System

EM™ Bokashi systems are a type of anaerobic system used extensively in Asia. More than three million Korean households use this composting method. The system consists of four buckets, two lids, and EM™ Bokashi mix, which is a blend of bran and so-called "Effective Microorganisms™," including lactic acid bacteria, yeast, photosynthetic bacteria, filamentous fungi, and actinomycetes that cause the compost to ferment. The Bokashi mix can be purchased separately and used in other brands of kitchen composters.

In the original Bokashi system, two of the buckets have holes drilled in the bottom, and the other two are solid. To start composting, place one drilled bucket inside a solid bucket and place your kitchen waste inside the top bucket. You can include any scraps, cooked or raw, and can even include animal products. Sprinkle the scraps with the Bokashi mix to cover them and compress the mixture by hand to squeeze out any liquid into the bottom bucket. Replace the lid and make sure it is attached tightly to prevent oxygen from entering the compost and to prevent odors from seeping out.

After you fill the first set of buckets, begin using the second set. By the time the second set is full, the contents of the first set are usually ready to be buried in the ground or added to an outdoor compost heap. By this time, the meat products will have broken down enough to be added to the outdoor heap without attracting pests. You can dilute the liquid from the bottom bucket and use it as a compost tea to water plants. Some types of kitchen composters come with a tap on the side so you can drain off the water as needed.

Electric systems

There are several brands of electric-powered compost systems on the market. This kind of system uses an electric motor to stir the compost and uses heating elements to warm the compost. Because the compost is artificially heated, this kind of system can usually consume products that you cannot put in outdoor systems, such as meat, small bones, and animal waste.

NatureMill, Inc., (**www.naturemill.com**) makes a sleek and modern-looking indoor composter that can handle up to 120 pounds of waste per month. This composter currently retails for $299 to $399, depending on the model you choose. It is 20 inches high by 20 inches deep by 1 foot wide and can fit easily into a kitchen cabinet. It can also be used outdoors in a sheltered location where the electrical connection is safe from the elements. The NatureMill composter heats and stirs the compost internally and has a container in the bottom that catches the finished compost as it is made. To use it, the manufacturer recommends purchasing a "booster mix" of microorganisms and coir bricks, which are bricks of coconut fibers. These are mixed with the compost to provide a carbon source. This type of composter can handle meat, fish, and dairy scraps and can also compost pet waste and kitty litter.

GreenGood® (**www.greengood.com**) makes an indoor "in-vessel" composter. The residential version of the machine can accept slightly more than 4 pounds of food waste each day. It heats the waste and mixes it with bacteria-laden sawdust. After it ferments, the bulk of the waste is reduced by 95 percent. The gases generated by the bacteria are filtered and the resulting water and carbon dioxide by-products are released through a tube to the outdoors. The microbes in this kind of system are extremely hearty and can tolerate acidic and neutral environments (0 to 8 on the pH scale). They can tolerate up to 19 percent salinity and can decompose fish, meat, poultry bones, and animal waste. The company also makes larger composters for use by restaurants, schools, hotels, and even remote islands. The home version was not available for sale in stores at the time of this writing, but interested individuals may contact Sara Estep, GreenGood's business development director, at 704-784-0012, for ordering information.

The selection of systems discussed in this chapter should provide an idea of the wide range of available composting options. One of them could be the tool you need to help you start composting and making wonderful soil amendments for your plants.

CASE STUDY

Sara Estep
Amateur composter
Concord, North Carolina
Business Development Director
www.greengood.com

I have been composting for a couple of months using an in-vessel compost system manufactured by Green Good®. The machine is quite clean and efficient with minimal odors, but sometimes there are items that are not fully composted, and I have to filter them out.

I use the finished compost on my lawn and garden. I enjoy knowing that I have diverted pounds of food waste from the landfill and turned it into nutrients and vitamins for my lawn that are natural for our planet.

My son is 4 years old, and he loves the thought of recycling and composting. He does not completely understand yet the concept of doing it, but loves to be my helper. This is a motivation for me to do it because it inspires him so much.

CHAPTER 10

TROUBLESHOOTING

Although composting is a simple and relatively safe activity, you should take some precautions to avoid disease, pests, and problems with neighbors. As with any gardening activity, you should ensure that you have the correct gear. For outdoor composting, you should wear sturdy footwear and gloves to protect your feet and hands. When working outdoors, a good hat and sun block is also recommended. Proper and careful use of your tools (rakes, pitchforks, garden spades, hoes, etc.) will also go a long way to keep you healthy and free from injury. The advice below deals with specific illnesses and problems that might arise while composting.

Diseases

Composting puts you in close touch with the soil and all the organisms, good and bad, which live in it. While most of these bacteria and fungi are harmless to healthy people, a few that can cause serious illness. If you have a compromised immune system for any reason, you also should take extra precautions to ensure that you stay healthy enough to enjoy the fruits of your labor.

Farmer's lung

Farmer's lung is a respiratory infection similar to pneumonia.

Cause. Farmer's lung is caused by inhaling bacterial and fungal spores that are present in rotten hay, sugarcane, or mushroom compost. The actinomycetes that are so good at composting paper and that give clean healthy soil its distinctive smell are the culprit here. You can identify them in compost by their gray or white webs that resemble fungal strands.

Prevention. Wear a dust mask while working with rotted hay or dry compost because the spores can quickly become airborne as you stir and turn the compost pile. Change and wash your clothes after working with compost.

Treatment. Farmer's lung is treated with antibiotics.

Histoplasmosis

Histoplasmosis is a respiratory infection.

Cause. It is caused by Histoplasma capsulatum, a fungus found in bat and bird manure. It is common in soil, especially throughout the Midwest and the upper South (Kentucky, North Carolina, Tennessee, Virginia, and West Virginia). While this fungus does not pose a problem for most healthy people, inhalation of large quantities can cause illness.

Prevention. Wear a dust mask when working with bird manure or bat guano.

Treatment. Histoplasmosis is treated with anti-fungal medication.

Legionnaires' disease

Legionnaires' disease is a respiratory infection similar to pneumonia.

Cause. The common type of Legionnaires' disease is associated with the bacteria *Legionella longbeachae* and is affiliated with air conditioning and cooling systems. This bacterium is found in some commercial potting soils in Japan and Australia. The first American cases of disease this bacterium caused were found in 2000.

Prevention. Wear a dust mask when working with commercial potting soils. Also, ensure that your compost reaches a temperature of at least 110 degrees to kill the bacterial spores. Always moisten potting soil and dry compost with water before using it to reduce the likelihood of inhalation.

Treatment. *Legionella longbeachae* infection is treated with antibiotics or respiratory therapies.

Paronychia

Paronychia is a painful infection of the area surrounding the fingernail. It can manifest as redness, swelling, or blisters.

Cause. Variations of this disease include fungal, bacterial, and candidal, all of which can infect gardeners. It is more common in people who have damp hands for much of the day and in those with diabetes.

Prevention. Always wear clean, dry gloves that are in good repair. Never wear wet gloves or gloves with holes in the fingertips. If you have open wounds on your fingers, including hang nails, paper cuts, and other minor injuries, cover the wounds and wear latex or nitrile gloves under your gardening gloves.

Treatment. Treatment depends on the type of infection. Fungal infections will be treated with anti-fungal medication, and bacterial infections can respond to warm water soaks several times a day. Antibiotics may be prescribed and, if infection is severe, the skin may be lanced to drain pus.

Tetanus

Tetanus, also called lockjaw, is a disease that causes a painful tightening of muscles all over the body. It is fatal in 10 to 20 percent of cases.

Cause. Tetanus infection results from exposure to the *Clostridium tetani* bacteria, which can occur any time an open wound is exposed to the soil.

Prevention. A vaccine is available, and adults should receive a booster shot every ten years. If you get a cut or puncture while working outside, get vaccinated right away to ward off the disease.

Treatment. If caught early enough, tetanus can be treated with immune globulin injections. Bed rest is advised, and if spasms become severe, the patient may be sedated, medically paralyzed, or placed on a respirator. Antimicrobial drugs can be used to eradicate the bacteria.

Toxoplasmosis

Toxoplasmosis is a disease that presents with symptoms like a mild flu and sometimes has no symptoms at all. According to the U.S. Centers for Disease Control and Prevention, it is the third leading cause of death attributed to food-borne illness in the United States. While the disease is normally not a problem for healthy people, pregnant women can pass the disease along to their fetuses, causing blindness and nervous system disorders. People with suppressed immune function can also catch the disease.

Cause. Toxoplasmosis is spread by the parasite *Toxoplasma gondii*, which is sometimes present in cat feces, meat, and unwashed produce. People can be exposed to this parasite if they handle or compost cat litter, or eat improperly cooked meat or unwashed produce.

Prevention. You can avoid catching toxoplasmosis by avoiding cat litter and not including it in your compost. If there are feral or outdoor cats in your neighborhood, always wear gloves and wash your hands well after gardening. Always carefully wash all fruit and vegetables before consuming them.

Treatment. Healthy people usually do not require treatment as their immune system kills off the parasite. Those who do develop an infection are treated with the drugs pyrimethamine and sulfadiazine, plus folinic acid (which is a form of folate similar to folic acid). The parasite cannot always be completely eradicated and those with suppressed immune function may sometimes require treatment for the rest of their lives.

Common Compost Problems and Solutions

While less traumatic than an illness, problems with your compost can cause you grief. A number of things can potentially go wrong with a compost pile. For example, it may begin to smell bad and may attract vermin. It may fail to heat up as it should, or may heat up only in the middle. Each of these problems has a simple solution.

Problem	Possible Causes	Solutions
Animal pests	If a compost pile attracts vermin such as rats, raccoons, and possums, it is most likely because animal products such as fat, bones, or meat have been introduced into the compost.	Switch to a type of compost system such as an electric system that heats the material artificially, a digester system where the waste is buried underground, or a completely enclosed system like a Green Johanna™ that can decompose meat and animal products. Try to bury animal products in the middle of the pile where they will be less likely to attract vermin, but this will not discourage determined animals. Switch to an enclosed and elevated tumbler system. Leave out meat and animal products altogether.
Odor	If a compost pile smells bad, it is probably due to poor maintenance: either the wrong balance of materials is being used, or the pile is not being turned often enough to allow oxygen to flow into the material. An offensive odor can also occur if the compost is allowed to get too wet.	Make sure the compost is properly aerated. Turn it frequently until it dries out. Ensure the compost is not too wet. Add brown material to soak up the liquid, if necessary. Make sure that you are maintaining a proper balance of green and brown materials in the compost.

Problem	Possible Causes	Solutions
Flies	Flies are commonly attracted to compost piles. They eat the compost and lay their eggs in it. While they do introduce beneficial bacteria to the compost, they can also use it as a breeding ground.	To prevent breeding by horseflies, houseflies, and mosquitoes, keep garbage covered and cover the top of an open compost pile with dry grass and leaves, flakes of hay or straw, or a piece of window screen to prevent these insects from landing and laying eggs. If fruit flies are a problem in an enclosed outdoor bin, leave the lid ajar for a few days. Beetles will soon move into the compost and eat the fly larvae, taking care of the problem for you. Never use pesticides in a compost bin because these poisons linger in the environment and will persist in the soil, possibly being taken up by food plants. If fruit flies are a problem in your kitchen where you are collecting food scraps, there are a few ways to get rid of them. Keep the scraps covered as much as possible. Buy fruit fly traps, such as those sold by garden supply companies. They usually come with an attractive box made of ceramic or soapstone and include replaceable traps that fit inside the box, out of sight. For a do-it-yourself method, try poking holes in a plastic bottle or small plastic tub with a lid. Bait the trap with apple cores, bits of banana, or other smelly fruit. Add enough water to make the fruit float and put a few drops of dish detergent in the water. The flies will drown because the detergent will break the surface tension of the water. Re-bait the traps daily until the flies are gone.
Ants	Ants may be attracted to an outdoor compost pile because it contains food. If the pile is too dry, they may try to take up residence in it.	To deter ants, make sure to keep the compost properly moist. Ants prefer to live in dry areas. If you do get an infestation, you can kill ants with Spinosad, which is an over-the-counter, biologically based insecticide. The bacteria in the insecticide are naturally occurring, and this product has been approved for use on USDA-certified organic produce, so it is safe to use in your compost or on your vegetable garden.

Problem	Possible Causes	Solutions
Pile not heating	A pile may fail to warm up if it lacks nitrogen, is too dry, needs to be turned, or is finished composting.	If the pile lacks nitrogen, add grass clippings, fresh manure, or blood meal. Mix the items in as well as you can and wait a few days, checking occasionally to see if it has warmed up. If the pile is too dry, water it. If the compost is compacted and the water is not sinking in, poke holes in the pile before watering it, and then mix the pile up to distribute the moisture. If the pile has already gone through one heating cycle, you will need to turn it before it will heat up again. Mix the materials well with a pitchfork or aerating tool. If the pile is done composting, which you can tell by the rich, dark appearance and earthy aroma, use it and make a new batch.
Pile is warm only in the middle	A pile that only gets hot in the middle is too small.	This occurs most often in piles or heaps, but can also happen in smaller containers. Add more material to create a larger pile, if possible, or resign yourself to having a slower compost pile.

Problems with Neighbors

Non-gardeners sometimes have an erroneous view of composting, thinking that it is a smelly, nasty business. This misunderstanding can cause problems between neighbors, but most people will see reason if you can educate them about composting. In fact, it might be a great opportunity to discuss starting a community compost club or shared garden. These myths might also make you hesitant to try composting. If that is the case, read this list of common myths about composting, and see if it changes your mind.

Addressing these issues before they become a problem will make your composting and gardening, not to mention relations with your neighbors, more pleasant. Here are some ideas for getting your neighbors to not just tolerate your composting, but also to join in the fun themselves.

- Offer to give them a free batch of compost. Yes, this will require some work on your part, but consider it an investment in neighborhood peace and quiet. Once your neighbors see what this free, natural resource does for their garden or flowers, they may decide composting is not so bad after all.

- Appeal to their better nature. Even the most jaded people care a little bit about nature. If your neighbor recycles, point out that composting is the ultimate form of recycling. If they drive an energy-efficient car, point out that composting can also help save the environment from further harm by keeping food and yard waste out of landfills.

- If they have children, point out that this is a healthy and fun way for kids to get involved in saving the earth. Offer to teach their kids how to compost either with your existing compost pile or on their own using worms.

- If your town or city does not already have a comprehensive composting program, start one. There is strength in numbers, and having an organized community composting group can help you find like-minded friends with whom you can share ideas and grow the group toward bigger and better things.

- If all else fails, build a fence. Good fences make good neighbors, and if they cannot see your compost pile, they may be less inclined to gripe about it. As an added benefit, the fence will add to your property value, and you can grow a row of beautiful, healthy compost-fed flowers along it.

How to Start a Community Composting Group

If you want to share what you have learned about composting, you might consider starting your own community composting group. Like any other effort, you will need two things above all — organizational ability and time. While composting at home is a leisurely process of gathering a small amount of scraps and waiting for them to break down, managing a group of people can be more difficult. If you do not have the people management and project management skills to do this on your own, team up with a friend who has the skills you need.

A fall harvest from a community garden.

First, you need to answer some questions.

- What kind of composting will you do? If you want to encourage people to compost at home, have several options ready to suggest to them. Some people might enjoy vermicomposting while others will prefer the enclosed bin, the three-bin method, or the trench method. Be prepared to teach the members of your composting group each method. Perhaps your core group of organizers could divide the task and each master a different kind of composting. Teaching is the best way to learn any task, and you could hold a hands-on composting day in your garden for people interested in the method you have mastered.

- If you plan to compost on a large scale by collecting waste from your neighbors, you will have to decide where the compost will be made. You will need a location where you are allowed to pile up domestic waste from several households. Will this require permission? Find out from local authorities if you need a permit, and who issues the permit. If you live in a rural area, someone might be able to donate a few acres of their own land to the cause, but in small towns, you may need to make sure that you do not run afoul of zoning laws.

- Do you have someone with a truck who is willing to collect compost? You will have to schedule pick-up times and have rules about what can be included in the compost and what must be left out. You may also want people to use a particular kind of container that is easy for the collection crew to pick up and dump. Alternatively, you may want to have residents drop off compostable material at a designated site. Where will they bring it? When? In what sort of container? All this must be planned ahead of time and communicated to the people involved.

- How many people will you have in your composting group? The number of households you can support will depend on how much land you have available to compost on and how much waste each household can contribute. Of course, homeowners can continue to compost individually, so that might take some of the pressure off your group's burden.

Once you know how and where you will compost, how you will collect the waste, and how many households you can accommodate, you have to get the word out about your new composting plans. Advertise a group meeting in places where gardeners go, which can be the local feed store, hardware store, or community garden, if there is one.

You may also want to limit the group to people in your immediate neighborhood to make it more manageable rather than opening it to the entire town. Is there a neighborhood watch group, homeowners association, community center, or other local gathering place or group where you can easily spread the word? If you want a larger group of people, try putting up fliers at the library, grocery store, coffee shop, or other frequently visited locations to advertise your first meeting. But if you have the resources to run a larger group, by all means, go ahead and try it.

At that first meeting, you will want to make sure to communicate all the plans, gather ideas from the attendees, and schedule the next meeting. At all points, communication is vital. If people do not know what is happening or when events are occurring, they will not be able to contribute as well as they should. Regularly scheduled meetings will help keep people on track, but not everyone can make it to every meeting. A newsletter (emailed or in the form of a flier posted at an agreed-upon location) is one suggestion. You can also enlist the help of an Internet-savvy person to create a blog or website where people can stay up to date on happenings in the group. Whatever method you choose, be sure to ask for feedback from the members. They can tell you whether or not you are communicating in an effective manner.

After the initial planning and meeting, you will need to get down to work collecting waste and composting. You will need volunteers to collect the materials, build the compost piles, and turn the compost. Very large piles will require the use of heavy equipment, such as front-end loaders or back-hoes, to turn and mix the pile. You may be able to rent, lease, or borrow one, or perhaps have one donated to your group. While large piles can be turned by hand if you have a dedicated crew of people willing to lift a shovel on a regular basis, anything bigger than a standard backyard compost pile will probably need some kind of mechanical assistance to keep the job manageable.

By the time you need a bulldozer or backhoe to turn the compost pile, you are getting into large-scale compost management, which may or may not be your goal. An endeavor of that kind will require money — either from donations or through some kind of service fee — and now you are in a completely different realm, because running a business is outside the scope of this book. However, if you choose to do large-scale composting, you will not be alone. Several groups around the world have already made a head start in this direction. Below are some links to groups that have already done this in their own communities.

Community Composting Inc. (**www.communitycomposting.ca**) is a business in British Columbia, Canada, that provides services to make composting easy, clean, and affordable. It is owned and operated by Matthew Mepham and Kyle Goulet and was founded in 2005. Community Composting Inc. currently services more than 1,500 people in Victoria, British Columbia.

The Community Composting Network (**www.community compost.org**) is a group in the United Kingdom that supports and promotes the management and use of biodegradable resources. This organization of about 230 members is self-managed by an elected committee. The group provides many services, including networking between new and experienced composting groups, maintaining a lending library of composting books, acting as composting consultants, and keeping members informed via website, e-mail news list, directory of members, annual conferences, and training events.

Although there are a few things that can go wrong when composting, a few, very simple precautions can prevent them. Keeping safety in mind when working with tools, dirt, and unfamiliar equipment is the best way to remain healthy while happily composting.

CASE STUDY

Carrie Bennett
Amateur composter
Berkeley, California

I am an amateur composter. I completed Master Composter Training at StopWaste.Org of Alameda County (**http://www.stopwaste.org/?page=441**). It was a wonderful experience. I think many communities are making this kind of training available these days.

I compost because it is fun to dig around in the decomposing organic matter to see all the life it supports, both within the bin and after it is put to use in the yard. I also enjoy diverting waste from the landfill and putting it to better use on my own property. I use my finished compost around my plants, especially any that look like they are struggling for nutrition. I add the compost to the surface of the soil, then water to help it soak in. I also add compost to the soil when planting new plants.

I have a Biostack compost bin, which is about 1 cubic yard capacity. I compost a variety of kitchen and yard scraps. I occasionally poke or turn the compost, but generally take a very casual approach and let it do its own thing. I also have a brush pile for bigger, woodier scraps that will break down more slowly.

I used to keep a worm bin outside, but it was hard to keep the moisture level high enough during the long, dry summers. I now keep a worm bin inside at work. It is the Wriggly Wranch™ brand, stocked with red wiggler worms. I feed them kitchen scraps. I like that the worms have a stable temperature and environment, but people tend to set things on top of the worm bin, sometimes making it a hassle to get into the bin to feed them.

I really like almost everything about composting. It can be quite a good stress reliever to go outside, add scraps to the bin, turn or poke the contents, and observe the life forms. It eases my mind to see the cycle of life played out so serenely. My favorite things about composting are watching the critters in the bin and seeing something that started out as garbage transform into a valuable resource. The only downside is that my Biostack is in a part of the yard that can get quite muddy during the winter, and I do not like tracking the mud into the house.

I want everyone to know composting is easy, fun, and beneficial. Adding more of one or more of the four basic ingredients — browns (carbon-rich organic matter), greens (nitrogen-rich organic matter), water, and air — can easily solve any compost troubles.

CONCLUSION

T hroughout this book, we have discussed why you might want to compost and how to do it. By now you probably see kitchen scraps and yard waste not as garbage, but as ingredients you can use to create something wonderful — fertile soil amendments that will give you beautiful flowers, healthy vegetables, and a new connection to the cycle of life on earth. The collection and composting of what you formerly thought of as trash can be seen as participating in nature, helping it along for its own good and yours. Humans are not separate from nature, but a part of it, and must be caretakers of the earth and its resources.

Entire communities can get in on the composting action; it is not something that you have to do alone. You may live in a community where there is no central trash authority and no municipal compost pick up. In North America, many communities lack these services, especially in small towns and rural areas. Towns that do not compost either have to maintain landfills or have to pay to have waste trucked to landfills many miles away, sometimes in other states or countries.

An island that is well-known for its composting activity is Mackinac Island, Michigan. Mackinac is a small island less than 4 square miles in area. The entire island is a National Historic Landmark, and more than 80 percent of the island is preserved as a state park. Trash from the island is shipped to a landfill in Michigan, but recycling and composting is strongly encouraged for all of the islands' 500 or so residents. Residents and businesses sort their household waste into compostables, recyclables, and actual trash. The compostable material is mixed with horse manure, hay, and straw and is composted right on the island. The finished compost is then used in city gardens and sold to residents and businesses. Because there are almost no motor vehicles on the island (apart from the ambulance and the tractor at the compost facility) and people frequently travel by horse, there is a large amount of manure available for composting.

The composting program on Mackinac received a boost in visibility in 2007 when Mike Rowe from the Discovery Channel show *Dirty Jobs* visited and worked at the island's Solid Waste Handling Facility. In addition, the island's Grand Hotel was recently awarded a "Leader" certification by Green Lodging Michigan for its efforts at composting. The Green Lodging certification program is administered by the Michigan Department of Energy, Labor & Economic Growth. This voluntary program for hotels establishes environmental guidelines for the use of water, energy, and waste disposal and encourages the conservation of natural resources to prevent pollution.

In a press release from April 2009, Grand Hotel's superintendent of grounds Mary Stancik, said, "Anything you see on the grounds is dirt that we made ourselves. None of it is from anywhere else. Every single grass clipping, every weed, and every flower that is taken from the ground when the growing season is over goes into the compost pile."

According to Stancik, all the dirt on the grounds of the hotel came from the composting program. Every bit of greenery that is collected at the end of the season is composted and returned to the hotel grounds.

You can read more about Mackinac Island's efforts to compost here: **www.grandhotel.com/pdfs/grand-hotel-green-initiatives.pdf**.

We began our discussion with a quotation from Zen master Thich Nhat Hanh about how garbage becomes a rose, and a rose becomes garbage. We have seen how the rose does not have to become garbage, but can be transformed through the efforts of humans, insects, and microbes into tasty, nutritious vegetables and lush, beautiful flowers. If I leave you with one wish, it is that you will see everything in your life in a new light — not as an end product, but as a component of life itself. Everything is part of the whole that is just waiting to be put in its proper place to do what it needs to do.

APPENDIX A

MORE INFORMATION ON VERMICOMPOSTING

The following websites can give you additional information on vermicomposting.

This blog, titled "Worm Farming," contains an entry on the history of worms and discusses how they were once considered pests. **http://worm-farming.blogspot.com/2007/08/history-of-worms-and-worm-farming.html**

This news article talks about Justin Rogers, who began using vermicompost tea on his own potato fields and eventually ended up selling it to friends and neighbors. **www.chieftain.com/business/local/article_e2fad144-7d9e-11df-8155-001cc4c03286.html**

Red Worm Composting is the website of Bentley Christie, who calls himself "the Compost Guy." His website contains a variety of resources for vermicomposters including videos, a blog, a newsletter, and a business directory for vermicompost items. **www.redwormcomposting.com/**

Wiki How is an online, user-generated encyclopedia, similar to Wikipedia, which contains useful instructions on how to do many common tasks. These two articles contain instructions on building a vermicompost bin and making worm casting tea.
www.wikihow.com/Make-Your-Own-Worm-Compost-System
www.wikihow.com/Make-Worm-Castings-Tea

Vermicomposting Supplies

Wood Worm Farms is a website that sells vermicomposting worms, bins, and accessories.
www.woodwormfarms.com

Worms Wrangler manufactures, wholesales, and retails worm-related products worldwide.
http://wormswrangler.com

Wormfarm.com sells vermicomposting supplies for home, school, or office.
www.wormfarm.com

APPENDIX B

WHERE TO PURCHASE COMPOSTING ITEMS

Y ou can purchase composting supplies and accessories from a wide variety of places. Garden supply stores are the most obvious choice, but if there are none convenient, you can usually find the basics at a hardware store or a large home improvement store like Lowe's or Home Depot. Many small towns and rural areas have farm supply stores that will carry most of what you need, and smaller stores are often willing to special order items for you. Large stores such as Meijer or Walmart usually have garden centers in the spring and summer that carry most of what you will need to compost. If you live in an urban area or are looking for a very specialized item, the Internet is your best friend. A simple Web search for composting (or any other keyword) will bring up thousands of hits.

Where to Buy Compost Systems Mentioned in this Book

You can find composting systems at most garden centers and at many different online retailers. The specific composters mentioned in this book may be found at your local garden center or home improvement store, or you can order them from the websites listed below.

Earthmaker® composter — www.earthmaker.net
This New Zealand-developed aerobic composter, *discussed in Chapter 3*, can be purchased from a wide range of retailers, including Target, Meijer, Amazon.com, and others.

EM™ Bokashi — http://embokashi.com/ or www.compostma-nia.com/Bokashi-Kitchen-Composter-2-Full-Kits
This indoor fermenting composter is discussed in Chapter 8. The EM™ Bokashi site has general information about the composter, and the Compost Mania site sells the full kits.

NatureMill — www.naturemill.com
NatureMill is one brand of indoor electric composter discussed in Chapter 8. It can make compost in two weeks, and certain brands of this composter feature a foot pedal for hands-free composting.

GreenGood® — www.greengood.com
GreenGood® is another brand of indoor electric composter discussed in Chapter 8. They are not currently available for retail sale. Contact Sara Estep, GreenGood's Business Development Director, at 704-784-0012 for ordering information.

Solar Cone or Green Johanna™ — www.solarcone.net
Green Cone Solar Digester systems and the Green Johanna™ composter are discussed in Chapter 3. These are both outdoor systems that will require a small amount of yard space.

APPENDIX C

THE COMPOSTING COMMUNITY

As with any new endeavor, when you start composting for the first time, it is normal to have many questions. Where can you get supplies in your area? Where can you get free compost ingredients? What kind of pests should you be on the lookout for? If you are lucky, there will be an established group of composters in your town that can give you answers. But if you cannot locate like-minded folks, you can always turn to the Internet. You can research every detail of composting and read scientific articles about it. You can also socialize with other composters.

This Appendix provides two lists. One is a list of informational sites where you can learn all the basics of composting and glean some of the more esoteric facts about it, and the other is a list of garden-related message boards and online forums. These groups form a community of compost enthusiasts from all over the world. If reading dry scientific information is not giving you the information and interactivity that you need, you can turn to these forums and ask your questions of people who are active and experienced in composting.

Informational Sites

Each U.S. state and territory has a branch of the Cooperative Extension System. This system is responsible for non-credit educational and outreach activities in the communities it serves. One thing that most extension services provide is agricultural information specific to your state. Following is a list of the extension services sorted by state that provide information on composting and gardening. Each site may also have their information broken down by county.

Alabama	**www.aces.edu/counties**
Alaska	**www.uaf.edu/ces**
American Samoa	**www.amsamoa.edu**
Arizona	**http://extension.arizona.edu**
Arkansas	**www.uaex.edu/findus/county_offices. htm**
California	**http://ucanr.org**
Colorado	**www.ext.colostate.edu/cedirectory/ countylist.cfm**
Connecticut	**www.extension.uconn.edu**
Delaware	**http://ag.udel.edu/extension/index.php**
District of Columbia	**www.udc.edu/cooperative_extension/ coop_ext.htm**

Florida	**http://solutionsforyourlife.ufl.edu**
Georgia	**www.caes.uga.edu/extension/office.cfm**
Guam	**www.uog.edu**
Hawaii	**www.ctahr.hawaii.edu/ctahr2001/ Counties/offices.asp**
Idaho	**www.uidaho.edu/ag/extension**
Illinois	**http://web.extension.uiuc.edu/state/ findoffice.html**
Indiana	**www.ces.purdue.edu/counties.htm**
Iowa	**www.extension.iastate.edu/Counties/ state.html**
Kansas	**www.ksre.ksu.edu/map.aspx**
Kentucky	**www.ca.uky.edu/county**
Louisiana	**www.lsuagcenter.com/en/our_offices/ parishes**
Maine	**http://extension.umaine.edu**
Maryland	**http://extension.umd.edu/gardening/ index.cfm**
Massachusetts	**www.umassextension.org/index.php/ in-your-community**
Michigan	**www.msue.msu.edu/portal/default. cfm?pageset_id=25744&page_ id=25770&msue_portal_id=25643**

Micronesia-Kolonia	www.comfsm.fm
Minnesota	www.extension.umn.edu/offices
Mississippi	http://msucares.com/counties/index.html
Missouri	http://extension.missouri.edu/regions
Montana	http://extn.msu.montana.edu/localoffices.asp
Nebraska	www.extension.unl.edu/web/Extension/officeslist
Nevada	www.unce.unr.edu
New Hampshire	http://ceinfo.unh.edu/Counties/Counties.htm
New Jersey	www.rcre.rutgers.edu/county
New Mexico	www.cahe.nmsu.edu/county
New York	www.ilr.cornell.edu/extension/locations.html
North Carolina	www.ag.ncat.edu/extension/locations.htm
North Dakota	www.ag.ndsu.nodak.edu/ctyweb.htm
Northern Marianas	www.nmcnet.edu
Ohio	http://extension.osu.edu/counties.php
Oklahoma	http://countyext.okstate.edu

Oregon	**http://extension.oregonstate.edu/ locations.php**
Pennsylvania	**http://extension.psu.edu/**
Puerto Rico	**www.uprm.edu/agricultura/sea/ newmap.html**
Rhode Island	**http://cels.uri.edu/ce**
South Carolina	**www.clemson.edu/extension**
South Dakota	**http://sdces.sdstate.edu/ces_website/ county_offices_bottom.cfm**
Tennessee	**www.utextension.utk.edu/offices/ default.asp**
Texas	**http://county-tx.tamu.edu**
Utah	**http://extension.usu.edu/cooperative/ index.cfm/cid.256**
Vermont	**www.uvm.edu/~uvmext**
Virgin Islands	**http://rps.uvi.edu/CES/index.html**
Virginia	**www.ext.vt.edu/offices**
Washington	**http://ext.wsu.edu/locations/ countyMap.html**
West Virginia	**www.wvu.edu/%7Eexten/depts/county. htm**
Wisconsin	**www.uwex.edu/ces/cty**
Wyoming	**http://ces.uwyo.edu**

The U.S. Composting Council, whose website can be found at **www.compostingcouncil.org**, is a national, non-profit trade and professional organization that promotes recycling organic materials using composts. The council has an educational arm and an online forum. You must apply to become a member.

Community Sites

As with every other hobby or interest, chances are you can find composters on the Internet. They can be found in places as diverse as LinkedIn (**www.LinkedIn.com**), the social networking site for professionals; Facebook (**www.facebook.com**), the social networking for everyone from teenagers to grandmas; and dedicated gardening forums. Below is a list of forums where composting enthusiasts gather to discuss different strategies for getting the most compost for the least amount of effort. They often discuss other green issues, such as recycling, re-use of materials, and a wide variety of related topics.

If you have never used an online forum before, it is a good idea to familiarize yourself with the rules of each forum. Here are some general guidelines to follow for any online forum site:

- Lurk for awhile before diving in. "Lurking" on a forum means reading several posts and getting a feel for the place. Some forums are very formal in nature and have a lot of rules about what you can and cannot post, while some are more free-wheeling. Take a few minutes, or preferably a few hours, to read over a selection of posts before composing your own.

- Read the "sticky" posts. Most online forums have items called "stickies." These posts are always visible at the top of a given forum. They usually contain the forum rules and guidelines and often contain a list of frequently asked questions. Sometimes you can find your answer in the sticky without bothering anyone with a question that has been asked several times.

- Most forums have FAQs, or frequently asked question lists. Always scan this list to see if anyone else has answered your question.

- Introduce yourself. Most forums have a thread that is designated specifically for people to introduce themselves. This helps the other members get to know you and provides a way for new members to scan the interests and knowledge of existing members.

- If you have knowledge, do not be shy about chiming in. A forum is a community, and a community grows richer if everyone participates. You may be new to composting, but if you have read this book, you already know a lot more than the average newbie. So, go ahead and offer an opinion or start a discussion. It could lead to a completely new group of friends.

The forums below were active as of July 2010.

- Facebook (**www.facebook.com**) is a social networking site with millions of users. Although most people use Facebook for socializing, there are informational groups on Facebook, including a few that are made up of folks interesting in composting. You must join Facebook and set up a profile in order to visit these groups. They include groups such as Garden Organic Master Composters, Compost toilets are the future, and others. A group search on "composting" should turn up several groups.

- Garden Web, found at **www.gardenweb.com**, bills itself as "The Internet's Home and Garden Community." The site provides information on every aspect of gardening and runs a host of different discussion forums, including one specifically for the discussion of compost, soil, and mulch, which can be found at **http://forums2.gardenweb.com/forums/soil**.

- Helpful Gardener Gardening Forum, found at **www.helpfulgardener.com**, hosts a wide variety of gardening-related forums. The compost forum can be found at **www.helpfulgardener.com/phpBB2/viewforum.php?f=35**.

- How to Compost, found at **www.howtocompost.org**, has a stated goal of becoming "the best resource on the Internet for composting information." While this site does not host a discussion forum, it does offer a wide selection of links on various aspects of composting and vermicomposting.

- LinkedIn (**www.linkedin.com**) is a professional social networking site designed to connect people based on whom they have worked with and know professionally. In order to access the groups on LinkedIn, you must join and set up a profile. Once you are logged into LinkedIn, you can do a search for groups related to composting. As of this writing, there are eight different compost-related groups including Compost Network, Food Waste Recycling, Compost Tahoe, and Buy Compost.

- The Dirt Doctor is the website of Howard Garrett. Garrett is a landscape architect, author, columnist, and radio host. The website has an active composting forum at **www.dirtdoctor.com/newforum/root/composting-forum-f1.html**.

- The Garden of Oz is a vermicomposting and regular composting forum on the Ning network. Ning is an online service that lets anyone create their own social network. There are Ning networks for almost any interest. You can find Garden of Oz at **www.gardenofoz.org/forum**.

- Vermi Forum is a forum all about vermicomposting and can be found at **http://vermiforum.com**.

- The Holistic Agriculture Library is a website that provides an extensive list of books on composting and gardening. **www.soilandhealth.org/01aglibrary/01aglib welcome.html**

GLOSSARY

Actinomycetes. Anaerobic filamentous bacteria that exist in healthy soil. Filamentous means that they look like filaments — long threads. They give garden earth its characteristic fresh, clean smell. In a compost pile, they form extensive webs of white or gray strands that resemble fungus. Do not inhale the spores of the actinomycetes as this can cause Farmer's Lung.

Activators. Substances that can help the composting process begin, but they are not necessary in most cases. There are many products on the market that claim to help start the composting cycle by introducing beneficial bacteria, enzymes, and hormones.

Aeration. The process of introducing air into a substance such as compost tea. Aeration helps keep microbes alive so that they can reproduce.

Aerobic. Creatures or processes that require oxygen. Aerobic bacteria are the foundation of a hot, active compost pile.

Anaerobic. Creatures or processes that do not require oxygen. Anaerobic bacteria cause organic waste to rot and putrefy. They can also give off toxic gases such as ammonia and are the cause of smelly compost piles.

Azobacteria. These bacteria live in soil and make nitrate nitrogen, which is required in large quantities for vegetables — especially corn, which needs between 120 and 160 pounds of nitrates per acre. They consume humus and require a balance of minerals — including calcium — and thrive where there is a pH level between 5.75 and 7.25.

Compost Sifter or Compost Screener. A wooden box with a metal screen attached to the bottom. Simply put handfuls of compost into the sifter and shake it lightly from side to side. The finished compost will pass through the screen, and the large pieces will remain in the filter so you can return them to the bin, where they can decompose further.

Compost Tea. A solution made of finished compost and water. Just like compost, it is full of healthy microbes and

nutrients, and because it is in a liquid form, plants can absorb it quickly. Compost tea can be aerated using aquarium pumps and other means.

Composting. The process of breaking organic matter down into its primary components so the resulting humus — the rich, dark organic soil made of decomposed plant and animal matter — can be used to fertilize plants and amend the soil.

Crop. An enlarged portion of the gullet that exists in birds, worms, and some insects.

Damping Off. A disease of new plantings and seedlings that can affect seeds before they sprout, cause them to wither as they sprout, or to fall over and die after sprouting. Compost helps prevent this disease and, thus, is a good additive to soils that will be used to sprout new seeds.

Downy Mildew. A type of fungal infection that affects plants such as grapevines, roses, and a variety of other ornamental and vegetable plants. Characterized by spots of gray, brown, purple, or white fungus, downy mildew will ruin leaves, flowers, and fruit of affected plants. Compost helps prevent this disease and, thus, is a good additive to soils that will be used to grow ornamental or vegetable plants. Plants that are affected should be disposed of properly and not put into your compost or municipal waste system because this can spread the disease.

Foliar fertilizer. A substance that is sprayed directly onto the foliage — leaves and stems — rather than on the soil. Compost tea can be used in this manner.

Grading. The process of leveling the ground so that it slopes smoothly in one direction or the other. This may be done to provide proper drainage of a compost heap or to allow rain and snow melt to run off away from a house. You can do this with a shovel and rake or with a tractor with a blade, depending on how much soil you need to move.

Humanure. Human fecal matter that has been composted. The method for doing this is not described in this book, but the resources section contains a link for the Humanure Handbook, and many resources can be found on the Internet.

Humus. Rich, dark organic soil matter made of decomposed plant and animal material.

Inoculants. Bacterial- or nitrogen-based additives that can be used to kick start the composting process. The nitrogen-based type is useful if you do not have enough green plant materials or if you are trying to produce a very hot compost pile very quickly. The bacterial type is useful if you do not have mature compost or other sources of bacteria to add to the compost. Inoculants are not required to make compost.

Lignin. Lignin is a fibrous plant compound found mostly in paper. It takes a long time for lignin to break down in a compost pile, so adding too much of it is not a wise thing to do unless you balance it with nitrogen-containing items.

Mesophilic bacteria. Bacteria that thrive at relatively low temperatures in the compost pile. They begin to take over when the temperature is between 70 degrees and 90 degrees.

Microorganisms. Also called microbes, microorganisms are any bacteria, fungi, or other organism not visible to the naked eye. They are vital to the composting process because without them the compost material will not break down into its component parts.

NPK ratio. NPK is shorthand for nitrogen, phosphorous, and potassium found in various kinds of fertilizers and soil enhancement products. The initials come from the chemical symbols for each of the nutrients — nitrogen is N, phosphorous is P, and potassium is K. Fertilizers are labeled with a series of three numbers that indicate the relative amount of nitrogen, phosphorous, and potassium in the given fertilizer. For example, a 5-10-5 fertilizer contains five parts nitrogen, ten parts phosphorous, and five parts potassium.

Peat. A non-renewable substance formed from partially decomposed moss, typically sphagnum moss, peat develops over centuries in wet boggy areas and swamps. Peat is used as a soil amendment and is harvested and sold commercially. Compost can replace the need for peat in gardening.

Pernicious weeds. Fast-growing, invasive, and destructive to other plants, weeds like thistle, bindweed, morning glory, and Bermuda grass are common examples of weeds that are generally considered pernicious. Often, they are non-native species, so the kind of weeds considered pernicious in one area may be tolerated in other states or countries.

pH. The measurement of the relative acidity or alkalinity of a given substance.

pH meter. An instrument with a probe that you insert into damp earth to measure the pH of that particular area, a pH meter costs about $25 and is available at most garden supply stores or online.

Post-hole digger. An implement used for digging holes for posts, it consists of two shovel-like blades hinged together and attached to a pair of long handles.

Potash. Also known as potassium carbonate, potash is a by-product found in wood ash that is used in gardening as a component of fertilizer.

Potato Blight. Also called late blight, this disease caused the Irish Famine by destroying potato crops. It also affects tomatoes. The disease begins as fuzzy green or brown fungal spots on the leaves and stem and can eventually cause the stem to collapse. Using compost in your garden can help prevent this disease. Affected plants should be disposed of properly and not put into your compost or municipal waste system as that can spread the disease.

Powdery Mildew. A fungal infection that affects both houseplants and outdoor plants, including fruit trees, roses, lilacs, and others, the disease manifests as several white powdery spots that gradually join together to form a mat of fungus. The areas of the plant where the fungus grows die off, sometimes killing or severely harming the entire plant.

Using compost in your garden can help prevent this disease. Affected plants should be disposed of properly and not put into your compost or municipal waste system because they can spread the disease.

Protozoa. Single-celled microorganisms that aid in the digestion and decomposition of compost materials.

Pyschrophilic bacteria. These bacteria flourish in cooling compost. They can live in temperatures between 0 and 65 degrees.

Rototiller. A landscaping implement with engine-powered, rotating blades used to lift and turn over soil.

Springtails. Tiny insects (usually 1 to 2 millimeters long, but sometimes up to 6 millimeters, or about ¼ inch) that spring or jump when disturbed, they are usually white, but can be other colors. They eat plants, pollen, and other small particles. They are usually beneficial to a worm bin because they help compost the food. They also can be found in outdoor compost piles from time to time. They like a moist environment.

Surfactants. Substances that help compost tea, pesticides, and other liquid sprays cling to leaves by breaking the surface tension of the liquid. This causes the liquid to form a sheet over the leaves rather than forming little droplets, which are not as effective at transferring their ingredients to the plant.

Taproots. The large, central roots of some plants that grow straight down with smaller roots branching off it. Think of a carrot, and you have the general idea.

Thermophilic bacteria. Bacteria that thrive at relatively high temperatures in the compost pile. They begin to take over when the temperature is between 113 degrees and 176 degrees.

They produce enzymes that are very efficient at decomposing protein, pathogens, weed seeds and roots, and other harmful items in the compost pile.

Tilling. The process of digging the soil, either to loosen up a thick clay soil or to introduce a soil amendment such as compost.

Vermicomposting. The process of making compost using worms. *See Chapter 7 for more information on vermicomposting.*

Bin Suppliers	
Hoops and Square Bins	**Contact**
C.E. Shepherd Company, Inc. P.O. Box 9445 Houston, TX 77261-9445	Phone: (713) 928-3763 Fax: (713) 928-2324
Clean Air Gardening 2266 Monitor Street Dallas, TX 75207	Phone: (214) 819-9500 Fax: (214) 853-4360 E-mail: sales1@cleanairgardening.com **www.cleanairgardening.com**
Covered Bridge Organic P.O. Box 91 Jefferson, OH 44047	Phone: (440) 576-5515 Fax: (440) 576-2467
The Green Culture ® 32 Rancho Circle Lake Forest, CA 92630	Phone: 877-20-GREEN Fax: 949-360-7864 **www.composters.com**
Green Line Products 1280 Finch Avenue West Suite 413 North York, Ontario CANADA M3J 3K6	Phone: (416) 667-9396 Fax: (416) 667-8033 E-mail: greenlin@idirect.com
Nature's Backyard, Inc. 585 State Road North Dartmouth, MA 02747	Phone: (800) 853-2525 or (508) 992-0404 Fax: (508) 992-0875 E-mail: compost@ici.com

Bin Suppliers	
Hoops and Square Bins	**Contact**
RPM 2829 152nd Avenue NE Redmond, WA 98052	Phone: (800) 867-3201
The WILMARC Company 1217 W. Main Street P.O. Box 8 Thorntown, IN	Phone: (317) 436-7089 Fax: (317) 436-2634
Cones and Boxes	**Contact**
Clean Air Gardening 2266 Monitor Street Dallas, TX 75207	Phone: (214) 819-9500 Fax: (214) 853-4360 E-mail: sales1@cleanairgardening.com **www.cleanairgardening.com**
Gardener's Supply Co. 128 Intervale Road Burlington, VT 05401	Phone: (800) 955-3370 **www.gardeners.com**
Green Composting Garden.Com 59256 Road 225, Suite 103 North Fork, CA 93643	Phone: (559) 877-7083 Fax: (800) 624-9490 E-mail: support@greencompostinggarden.com **www.greencompostinggarden.com**
Green Cone Distributors P.O. Box 866 Menlo Park, CA 94026	Phone: (415) 552-6367 Retail: (415) 365-8637
The Green Culture ® 32 Rancho Circle Lake Forest, CA 92630	Phone: 877-20-GREEN Fax: 949-360-7864 **www.composters.com/**
Nutri-Cube Yard Composter 2740 32nd Avenue South Minneapolis, MN 55406	Phone: (612) 721-4456
Stackables	**Contact**
The Green Culture ® PO Box 1684 Laguna Beach, CA 92652	Phone: In the US, 800-233-8438 Int'l callers, 949-643-8795 Fax US: 800-480-8270 Fax Int'l: 949-643-3749

Stackables	Contact
Plastopan 812 East 56th Street Los Angeles, CA 90001	Phone: (213) 231-2225
Smith & Hawken Municipal Sales 117 East Strawberry Drive Mill Valley, CA 94941	Phone: (415) 383-4415

Tumblers	Contact
Clean Air Gardening 2266 Monitor Street Dallas, TX 75207	Phone: (214) 819-9500 Fax: (214) 853-4360 E-mail: sales1@cleanairgardening.com **www.cleanairgardening.com**
Gardener's Supply Co. 128 Intervale Road Burlington, VT 05401	Phone: (800) 955-3370 **www.gardeners.com**
Green Composting **Garden.Com** 59256 Road 225, Suite 103 North Fork, CA 93643	Phone: (559) 877-7083 Fax: (800) 624-9490 E-mail: support@greencompostinggarden.com **www.greencompostinggarden.com**
The Green Culture ® 32 Rancho Circle Lake Forest, CA 92630	Phone: 877-20-GREEN Fax: 949-360-7864 **www.composters.com**
Greener Sooner Inc. 11635 - 126 Street Edmonton, Alberta CANADA T5M 0R9	Phone: (780) 452-2194 Fax: (780) 454-5774 E-mail: greenersooner@v-wave.com
Mellinger's Inc. 2310 W. South Range Road North Lima, OH 44452	Phone: (800) 321-7444

BIBLIOGRAPHY

I nformation was gathered from the following books and websites.

13 Common Composting Myths – Earth911.com. (**http://earth911®. com/recycling/garden/composting/13-common-myths-of-composting/**) Accessed July 20, 2010.

Bailey, Kenny. *Environmental Concerns With Fertilizer Use*. North Carolina Cooperative Extension. March 25, 1999. (**www.ces.ncsu.edu/cumberland/fertpage/environ.html**) Accessed July 20, 2010.

Bugg, Robert L. *Earthworm Update*. UCDavis.edu, 1994. (**www.sarep.ucdavis.edu/worms/update.htm**) Accessed July 20, 2010.

Campbell, Stu. *Let it Rot*. North Adams, Massachusetts: Storey Publishing, 1998.

Centers for Disease Control and Prevention. Toxoplasmosis. (**www.cdc.gov/toxoplasmosis**) Accessed July 20, 2010.

Christchurch, New Zealand City Council. *The Compost Recipe for Success.* (**http://resources.ccc.govt.nz/files/ AGuideToGardenComposting-docs.pdf**) Accessed July 20, 2010.

Christian, Jeffrey. *Charts: Nutrient Changes in Vegetables and Fruits, 1951 to 1999.* CTV.ca. July 5, 2002. (**www.ctv.ca/servlet/ ArticleNews/story/CTVNews/20020705/favaro_nutrients_ chart_020705**) Accessed July 20, 2010.

City of Euless, Texas. *Compost-ology: The Science of Composting & Vermicomposting.* EulessTX.gov. (**www.eulesstx.gov/composting**) Accessed July 20, 2010.

City of Vancouver, British Columbia. *Case Study – Dog Waste Composting.* (**http://www.metrovancouver.org/about/ publications/Publications/DogWasteComposting.pdf**) Accessed July 20, 2010.

Composting Toilet World. (**http://compostingtoilet.org**) Accessed July 20, 2010.

Cureton, William Edward. *What are the Benefits of Aerated Compost Teas vs. Classic Teas?* Gardenweb.com. (**http://faq. gardenweb.com/faq/lists/organic/2002082739009975.html**) Accessed July 20, 2010.

Cureton, William Edward. *What do you do with animal manures in an organic garden?* GardenWeb.com. (**http://faq. gardenweb.com/faq/lists/organic/2003082510028156.html**) Accessed July 20, 2010.

Darwin, Charles, *The Formation of Vegetable Mould Through the Action of Worms.* London, United Kingdom: John Murray, 1881. (**http://charles-darwin.classic-literature.co.uk/formation-of- vegetable-mould/**) Accessed July 20, 2010.

Department of Homeland Security. *Secure Handling of Ammonium Nitrate Regulating the Sale & Transfer*. DHS.gov. (**www.dhs.gov/xlibrary/assets/chemsec_summit09_ ammoniumnitrateregulations.pdf**) Accessed July 20, 2010.

Ditchburn, John. *Straw Compost Bins*. UrbanFoodGarden.org. (**www.urbanfoodgarden.org/main/composting/composting--- straw-compost-bins.htm**) Accessed July 20, 2010.

EM Research Organization. (**www.emtechnologynetwork.org**) Accessed July 20, 2010.

Ebeling, Eric, ed., *Basic Composting: All the Skills and Tools You Need to Get Started*. Mechanicsburg, Pennsylvania: Stackpole Books, 2003.

EcoChem. *Chemical Fertilizer or Organic Fertilizer*. EcoChem.com. (**www.ecochem.com/t_faq9.html**) Accessed July 20, 2010.

EHow. *How to Sharpen a Machete*. EHow.com. (**www.ehow.com/ how_4549059_sharpen-machete.html**) Accessed July 20, 2010.

Eldorado Chemical. *Roles of The 16 Essential Nutrients In Crop Development*. EldoradoChemical.com. (**www.eldoradochemical.com/fertiliz1.htm**) Accessed July 20, 2010.

Extremely Green Gardening Co. (**www.extremelygreen.com**) Accessed July 20, 2010.

Gardner, Kate. *Compost: In the Bin, the Garden, and the Environment*. ComposterConnection.com. (**www.composterconnection.com/site/introduction.html**) Accessed July 20, 2010.

Garofalo, Michael, P. *The History of Gardening: A Timeline.* GardenDigest.com, March 19, 2003. (**www.gardendigest.com/ timel19.htm#Start**) Accessed July 20, 2010.

Global Healing Center. *Nutrient-Depleted Soil.* GlobalHealingCenter.com. (**www.globalhealingcenter.com/ nutrient-depleted-soil.html**) Accessed July 20, 2010.

Howard, Albert, and Wad, Yeshwant D. *The Waste Products of Agriculture: Their Utilization as Humus.* London, New York, Toronto, Melbourne, Bombay, Calcutta, Madras: Humphrey Milford, Oxford University Press, 1931. (**http://gutenberg.net. au/ebooks02/0200321.txt**) Accessed July 20, 2010.

Humanure Headquarters. (**www.humanurehandbook.com/**) Accessed July 20, 2010.

Huxley, Susan, ed. *50 Fast Garden Fixes.* Emmaus, Pennsylvania: Rodale Inc., 2008.

Juvonen R, Martikainen E, Schultz E, Joutti A, Ahtiainen J, Lehtokari M. *A battery of toxicity tests as indicators of decontamination in composting oily waste.* National Center for Biotechnology Information, October 2000. (**www.ncbi.nlm.nih. gov/pubmed/11023694**) Accessed July 20, 2010.

Kennard, Jim. *Can Manure or Compost Tea Replace Fertilizers?* FoodForEveryone.org, August 16, 2006. (**http:// foodforeveryone.org/faq/index.php?page=index_ v2&id=116&c=9**) Accessed July 20, 2010.

Khan, Saeed. *Study Reveals that Nitrogen Fertilizers Deplete Soil Organic Carbon.* University of Illinois College of Agricultural, Consumer, and Environmental Sciences, October 29, 2007. (**www.aces.uiuc.edu/news/internal/preview.cfm?NID=4185**) Accessed July 20, 2010.

National Cottonseed Products Association. *Beautiful Gardens with Cottonseed Meal A Slow Release Organic Fertilizer.* Cottonseed.com, 2002. (**www.cottonseed.com/publications/beautifulgardens.asp**) Accessed July 20, 2010.

National Wooden Pallet and Container Association. (**www.nwpca.com/SearchNew/ZipSearch.asp**) Accessed July 20, 2010.

Natural Environmental Systems. *Humic Acid's Role in Improving Soil Quality and Plant Growth.* (**www.naturalenviro.com/Article.php?ArticleSKU=humic-acid-role**) Accessed July 20, 2010.

Organic Garden Info. *Hoof and Horn Meal Organic Fertilizer.* (**www.organicgardeninfo.com/hoof-and-horn-meal.html**) Accessed July 20, 2010.

Piche, L.A. *Analysis: Apparent Nutrient Changes in Government Data for a Selection of Fruits & Vegetables: 1951 vs 1999.* CTV.ca, July 5, 2002. (**www.ctv.ca/servlet/ArticleNews/story/CTVNews/20020705/favaro_nutrients_analysis_020705?s_name=&no_ads=**) Accessed July 20, 2010.

Pleasant, Barbara, and Martin, Deborah L. , *Compost Gardening.* Emmaus, Pennsylvania: Rodale Inc., 2008.

Steege, Gwen, and Smittle, Delilah, eds. *The Complete Compost Gardening Guide.* North Adams, Massachusetts: Storey Publishing, 2008.

Recycle Works. *Feeding Your Worms.* (**www.recycleworks.org/compost/wormfood.html**) Accessed July 20, 2010.

Sasser J.N., and Carter, C.C., eds. *An Advanced Treatise on Meloidogyne.* Raleigh, North Carolina: North Carolina State University Graphics, 1985.

Scott, Nicky. *Composting: An Easy Household Guide*. White River Junction, Vermont: Chelsea Green Publishing Company, 2007.

Shreeves, Robin. *Compost vs Landfill: Does it Really Make a Difference?* SustainBlog.com, December 2, 2008. (**http://blog.sustainablog.org/compost-vs-landfill-does-it-really-make-a-difference/**) Accessed July 20, 2010.

Simplot. *Products: Ammonium Sulfate*. (**www.simplot.com/agricultural/plant/amm_sulfate2100.cfm**) Accessed July 20, 2010.

Soloman, Steve. *Organic Gardener's Composting: Chapter Nine: Making Superior Compost*. SoilandHealth.org. (**www.soilandhealth.org/03sov/0302hsted/030202/03020209.html**) Accessed July 20, 2010.

Texas A&M Agrilife Extension Service Composting Guide Chapter 1, The Decomposition Process. (**http://aggie-horticulture.tamu.edu/publications/landscape/compost/chapter1.html**) Accessed July 20, 2010.

Texas A&M Agrilife Extension Service Composting Guide Index. (**http://aggie-horticulture.tamu.edu/publications/landscape/compost**) Accessed July 20, 2010.

The AgriCultures Network. *Traditional Night Soil Composting Continues to Bring Benefits*. Leisa Magazine, June 2008. (**www.leisa.info/index.php?url=getblob.php&o_id=209104&a_id=211&a_seq=0**) Accessed July 20, 2010.

The Irish Peatland Conservation Council. *Gardening without peat*. IPCC.ie. (**www.ipcc.ie**) Accessed July 20, 2010.

The Organic Gardener. *Try making compost for seedlings and growing plants*. (**www.the-organic-gardener.com/making-compost.html**) Accessed July 20, 2010.

Thompson, Ken. *Compost: The Natural Way to Make Food for Your Garden*. New York: DK Publishing, 2007.

Tom Clothier's Garden Walk and Talk. *Damping Off*. (**http://tomclothier.hort.net/page13.html**) Accessed July 20, 2010.

United States Department of Agriculture. National Organic Program. (**www.ams.usda.gov/AMSv1.0/ams.fetchTemplateData.do?template=TemplateA&navID=NationalOrganicProgram&page=NOPNationalOrganicProgramHome&resultType=&topNav=&leftNav=NationalOrganicProgram&acct=nop**) Accessed July 20, 2010.

United States Environmental Protection Agency. *Composting*. EPA.gov. (**www.epa.gov/reg5rcra/wptdiv/solidwaste/recycle/compost/index.htm**) Accessed July 20, 2010.

United States Environmental Protection Agency. *Yard and Food Waste*. EPA.gov. (**www.epa.gov/region07/waste/solidwaste/yardandfood.htm**) Accessed July 20, 2010.

United States Food and Drug Administration. *Update on Ruminant Feed (BSE) Enforcement Activities*. FDA.gov, February 6, 2004. (**www.fda.gov/AnimalVeterinary/NewsEvents/CVMUpdates/ucm048448.htm**) Accessed July 20, 2010.

University of Illinois Extension. *Composting for the Homeowner: History of Composting*. (**http://web.extension.illinois.edu/homecompost/history.html**) Accessed July 20, 2010.

WebMD. *Pregnancy and Toxoplasmosis*. WebMD.com (**www.webmd.com/baby/toxoplasmosis**) Accessed July 20, 2010.

ABOUT THE AUTHOR

Kelly Smith is an author, quilter, and container gardener. Her previous works include the book *Open Your Heart with Quilting* (Dreamtime, 2008), the magazine article "Let's Play" in *Quilters Home* magazine (Nov./ Dec. 2008), and several quilt patterns for **QuiltingWeekly.com**. She is also the National Quilting Examiner for **Examiner.com** and writes about news and events of interest to quilters.

In addition to non-fiction writing, Kelly writes short stories and novels, and maintains a blog at **www.redheadedquilter.com**. You can follow her on Twitter at **www.twitter.com/quiltinredhead**.

INDEX